THE PIRATE
ECONOMY

Other books by Gary North

Marx's Religion of Revolution, 1968
An Introduction to Christian Economics, 1973
Unconditional Surrender: God's Program for Victory, 1981
Successful Investing in an Age of Envy, 1981
The Dominion Covenant: Genesis, 1982
Government by Emergency, 1983
The Last Train Out, 1983
Backward, Christian Soldiers?, 1984
75 Bible Questions Your Instructors Pray You Won't Ask, 1984
Coined Freedom: Gold in the Age of the Bureaucrats, 1984
Moses and Pharaoh: Dominion Religion Versus Power Religion, 1985
Negatrends, 1985
The Sinai Strategy: Economics and the Ten Commandments, 1986
Unholy Spirits: Occultism and New Age Humanism, 1986
Conspiracy: A Biblical View, 1986
Fighting Chance, 1986 [with Arthur Robinson]
Honest Money, 1986
Inherit the Earth, 1987
Dominion and Common Grace, 1987
Is the World Running Down?, 1987
Liberating Planet Earth, 1987
    (Spanish) *Teología de Liberación*, 1987

Books edited by Gary North

Foundations of Christian Scholarship, 1976
Tactics of Christian Resistance, 1983
The Theology of Christian Resistance, 1983
Editor, *Journal of Christian Reconstruction* (1974-1981)

THE PIRATE
ECONOMY

Gary North

American Bureau of Economic Research
Ft. Worth, Texas

ISBN 0-930462-25-4

Typesetting by Thoburn Press, Tyler, Texas

Published by
American Bureau of Economic Research
P. O. Box 8204
Ft. Worth, Texas 76124

TABLE OF CONTENTS

INTRODUCTION

Over the past few years, I have written numerous articles for my biweekly newsletter, *Remnant Review*, as well as having produced several books. Because many of these have dealt with basic economic theory, and strategies for investing and personal survival that grow out of economic theory, I have decided to rewrite them, update them, and republish them. This book is therefore a compilation of older essays, but I find that they are still as revelant as when I wrote them. In some cases, they are more relevant.

By putting them into a book format, I make available the information in a more digestible form. The cost of getting this information to readers is also much less, given the efficiencies of modern book production.

There is some repetition in the book because certain ideas have appeared on several occasions over a period of thirteen years. Nevertheless, some repetition is desirable if it drives home an important point into the memory of readers. I have always tried to keep from repeating myself too often, which is another reason for reprinting these essays. Subscribers to *Remnant Review* who have come on board recently probably don't understand fully what my economic presuppositions are and what strategies I have recommended in the past. The book will give new subscribers this perspective, and I will spare old-time subscribers the misery of going over familiar ground.

Unlike so many "How to Profit" books, this one focuses on underlying trends in the modern economy that tend to be ignored by more conventional economists and even newsletter writers. I am convinced that these contemporary presuppositions concerning the nature of government, the economy, and the legitimacy of wealth are crucially important. They are important for a proper understanding of the drift which has overtaken us politically and economically. But they are also important in providing us with confidence in what we are doing with our capital. I cannot stress this too much. We are taking steps in our personal and business lives that will be resented by others in the future, should others find out what we have done. It is imperative that every success-oriented investor have complete confidence in what he is doing, and this includes moral confidence. If you know what has to be done, but you neglect doing it because you think it's somehow immoral, or mean, or hard-hearted toward others, then you might as well never have known what to do. If anything, it will be worse, since you will be second guessing yourself once these crises hit the economy. "Why didn't I do that?" you'll say to yourself a hundred times. This book will make it easier for you psychologically to pursue a course of action that will help you to survive a whole series of economic and social disruptions.

This book has some special recommendations — investment tactics, as I call them — but I am concentrating on investment strategies here. I focus on an approach to investing, a kind of world-and-life view that rests on certain assumptions about the modern economy, including modern voters and politicians. What I want my readers to have after finishing this book is a comprehensive understanding of where this economy is going and what can be done to hedge themselves against it. Too many investors are going about their program in an ad hoc, haphazard manner. Their investments are not integrated into a well-thought-out framework. In short, too many investors have inconsistent investment portfolios. If you read and understand this book, you should be able to know where the weaknesses are in your present investment program.

Each chapter is a self-contained unit, but each fits into an integrated whole. Step by step, you will be given the fundamentals of economic analysis, as these fundamentals apply to the real world. I really believe that a thorough reading of this book will make it possible for readers to make investment decisions confidently, knowing that they are following the basic rules of successful investing in a pirate economy. You will become your own economic advisor, in effect. If the book increases your own personal confidence as you make key investment decisions, then it will have been worth the money, time, and effort spent in mastering these principles. Some of you will find that you have already taken the proper steps financially, but this book will give you a better understanding of what you have done, why it was right that you did it, and why you should not feel guilty when your decisions enable you to command resources in the future.

Guilt is a mental crippler, a source of emotional paralysis. This book is designed not only to provide you with accurate information concerning investing, but also the proper attitude toward financial success. If you do well, but needless guilt leads you to throw away your advantage, then your technical expertise in the investment world will have profited you little. This book is a handbook in guilt avoidance. It is a complement to David Chilton's important book, *Productive Christians in an Age of Guilt-Manipulators* (Box 8000, Tyler, TX: Institute for Christian Economics, 1981; $12.50). There are a lot of envious people in the world, and far too many religious specialists in guilt manipulation. You had better know how to defend yourself.

The Institute for Christian Economics is a tax-exempt, non-profit research organization. I'm the president. We publish several newsletters, books, position papers, tapes, and other materials. If you would like a free, six-month subscription to any (or all) of the newsletters, just write to the ICE with a $5.00 contribution and say that you bought and read *Pirate Economy.*

Institute for Christian Economics
P.O. Box 8000
Tyler, TX 75711

1

MAGIC, ENVY, AND
ECONOMIC UNDERDEVELOPMENT

Since the great depression of the 1930s, and especially since 1945, the concern of concerns among orthodox Keynesian planners has been economic growth. Believing they had created Western prosperity, they thought to export it to underdeveloped lands through massive giveaways. At some undefined point, these so-called "transfer payments" would enable the recipient nations to become productive. "Primitive" cultures could then become "modern."

But a major question still confronts the historians and economists: what factors contribute to economic growth? Why do some societies grow steadily, seemingly as a result of their own people's efforts, while others stagnate, despite foreign aid? The best answers have been offered by three scholars: an economist (P. T. Bauer), a political scientist (Edward Banfield), and a sociologist (Helmut Schoeck). Bauer, a professor at the London School of Economics, has published several important books on the topic of economic development, but by far his most comprehensive work is *Dissent on Development*, published by Harvard University Press in 1972. The key to economic development in a society, argues Bauer, is the character of the people. The presence of a socialist planning apparatus inhibits development, since it pours money into state-approved projects, bases its decisions on politics rather than economic returns, and acts as a scapegoat for personal failure ("the government did this to me"). But far more important is the attitude of the population:

Examples of significant attitudes, beliefs and modes of conduct unfavorable to material progress include lack of interest in material advance, combined with resignation in the face of poverty; lack of initiative, self-reliance and a sense of personal responsibility for the economic fortune of oneself and one's family; high leisure preference, together with a lassitude often found in tropical climates; relatively high prestige of passive or contemplat-

1

ive life compared to active life; the prestige of mysticism and of renuncia-
tion of the world compared to acquisition and achievement; acceptance of
the idea of a preordained, unchanging and unchangeable universe; emphasis on performance of duties and acceptance of obligations, rather than on
achievement or results, or assertion or even recognition of personal rights;
lack of sustained curiosity, experimentation and interest in change; belief in
the efficacy of supernatural and occult forces and of their influence over
one's destiny; insistence on the unity of the organic universe, and on the
need to live with nature rather than conquer it or harness it to man's needs,
an attitude of which reluctance to take animal life is a corollary; belief in
perpetual reincarnation, which reduces the significance of effort in the
course of the present life; recognized status of beggary, together with a lack
of stigma in the acceptance of charity; opposition to women's work outside
the household. (pp. 78-79).

These attitudes are primarily religious in nature. They are not
easily changed, and dollars alone, even billions of dollars annually,
are not likely to alter them significantly. A nation dependent on
another nation's largess is still caught in the trap of the occult. The
increased wealth is not a product of the recipient nation's planning
by conscientious men. It therefore will not teach men that wealth
stems from moral action and obedience to basic principles of conduct. The presence of attitudes such as those described in Bauer's
summary are the sign of "primitivism." Primitive external conditions
that persist in a culture through countless generations are a sign of
cultural degeneration—the wrath of God (Deuteronomy 8, 28).

Bauer's favorite example of a population that has pulled itself up
by its own bootstraps, without foreign aid, natural resources, or a system of massive central planning, is that little piece of rock south of
China, Hong Kong. Free trade, open entry to occupations, low taxes
(until quite recently), the right of profit, and an attitude favorable to
growth have combined to produce an economic miracle. Even the
Japanese cannot compete with them: American capitalists long ago
began screaming about the "unfair competition"—read: effective competition—of the inhabitants of this bit of rock. But Africa stagnates,
with its untold mineral wealth, or even declines economically.

The Unheavenly City

Edward Banfield's gem of a book, *The Unheavenly City* (1970),
earned him the wrath of most of the academic profession, as well as
the students of Harvard University. So continuous and bitter was

the student opposition that Banfield finally left "scholarly" Harvard for the University of Pennsylvania. What was the cause of such an outcry? Simple: Banfield had concluded that the economic backwardness of the ghetto is primarily the product of the chosen style of life of the majority of those who live in the ghetto. Most crucial, argues Banfield, is their conception of the future: their present-orientation is the key to understanding the concept of "lower class," not present income. Present income can rise later; it can be supplemented by income from other family members. But present-orientedness is internal. There is no imposed solution possible: no school program, with its system of endless written exams; no job training programs, that in 1967 were costing $8,000 per enrollee; no system of rehabilitation for hardened criminals. The problem is spiritual, moral, and cultural. White money changes only the level of activity in the ghetto, not its general direction.[1]

Both Bauer and Banfield have struck at the very heart of modern economic Liberalism. The simple world of environmentalism is a myth, they have concluded. So many dollars per capita of wealth redistribution on the part of civil governments means nothing. The key is internal. White middle-class bureaucrats, armed with their dollars and their survey forms, do not and cannot change anything. The old routine of "find a problem, cure a problem" is too simplistic; money and more public education are insufficient. White middle class bureaucrats have tried to transform men's lives and cultures by spending other people's money. It has been dollar diplomacy of the grossest kind: the attempt to buy people's minds. And it has failed, and failed miserably. The policies of Liberal reformism have constituted a massive, endless failure. The operating presupposition of their programs has been external environmentalism, and that principle is totally false. The problems are moral, not external. The slums are in people's hearts. Thus, concludes Nisbet in his lively review of Banfield's book, the old formula of Liberal bureaucracy has to be changed, from "Don't just sit there; do something!" to "Don't just do something; sit there!"[2]

---

1. Edward C. Banfield, *The Unheavenly City: The Nature and Future of Our Urban Crisis* (Boston: Little, Brown & Co., 1970). A second edition, *The Unheavenly City Revisited* (1974), answers his critics politely.

2. Robert A. Nisbet, "Urban Crisis Revisited," *Intercollegiate Review* (Winter, 1970-71), p. 7. Cf. Christopher De Muth, "Banfield Returns," *The Alternative* (Nov. 1974).

Educational Opportunity

Corroborating evidence has been produced in the field of public education. James S. Coleman supervised a major study of educational opportunity in the United States back in the mid-1960s. One estimate has placed it as the second most expensive social science research project in our history. Naturally, the Federal government funded it. The result was a lengthy report: *Equality of Educational Opportunity* (Government Printing Office, 1966). The data were startling. School facilities for black and white children, in any given region of the country, are about equal within that region, and equal in almost every statistically measurable respect. Per capita student expenditures are about the same. So is teacher training. The results have been published.[3] The primary conclusion of the Coleman Report and those studying its figures is simple: there is no measurable impact that public schools have had on eliminating or even modifying comparative achievement among students. Furthermore, the data indicate that no known changes in school inputs—teacher salaries, more expensive facilities, bigger school libraries—are likely to have any significant effect on student output. As the editors have written, "the central fact is that its findings were seen as threatening to the political coalition that sponsored it."[4] Understandably, it was ignored as long as possible.

What factors are important, according to the Coleman Report? Primarily, *family* inputs. Innate ability, peer group pressures, and community standards are also important. In short, there is no sign that anything short of radical reconstruction of the whole society would change the learning patterns of students, and there is no guarantee that even this would do anything but lower all performance to the least common denominator. Once again, the simplistic environmentalism of Liberal reformism has been thwarted, this time by its own methods of investigation. This, of course, has had no measurable effects on the calls for ever higher public school budgets. Now the reformers are convinced that public education has to start earlier, "before the lowered level of competence sets in."[5] If a century and a half of coercive public education has failed to meet its promised

---

3. Frederick Mosteller and Patrick Moynihan (eds.), *On Equality of Educational Opportunity* (New York: Random House, 1972).

4. *Ibid.*, p. 28.

5. *Ibid.*, p. 49.

goals, then there has to be more of it. All facts are interpreted in terms of the religious presuppositions of the investigators.

Envy

P. T. Bauer mentioned the belief in occultism as one of the cultural forces of economic retardation. Helmut Schoeck, the sociologist, has explored this in greater depth. His monumental study, *Envy*, has been conveniently ignored by most scholars. The facts he presents, however, are extremely important. His basic thesis is straightforward: envy against the wealth or achievements of others reduces the ability of individuals to advance themselves economically. Envy is not mere jealousy. It is not wanting the other man's goods for oneself. It is the outright resentment against anyone even possessing greater wealth — the desire to reduce another person's position even if this reduction in his wealth in no way improves the position of the envious person. Nowhere is envy more devastating in its effects than in so-called primitive cultures.

If a person of his family gets ahead of the accepted tribal minimum, two very dangerous things can easily take place. First, he will be suspected of being a wizard or a witch (which can be the same thing). Second, he can become fearful of being the object of the evil magic of others. As Schoeck writes, "the whole of the literature on the subject of African sorcery shows the envious man (sorcerer) would like to harm the victim he envies, but only seldom with any expectation of thereby obtaining for himself the asset that he envies — whether this be a possession or a physical quality belonging to the other."[6] Understandably, this envy is present only where there is *close social proximity* between the envious and the envied. It is always considered very difficult to bewitch a stranger with any success.[7]

The efficacy of demon magic is strong in these non-Christian cultures. The fear of magic is pervasive. Thus, the threat of its use against the truly successful man causes men with talents to conceal them from their fellows. Men become secretive about what they own. They prefer to attribute any personal successes to luck or fate, both impersonal.

"*Institutionalized envy*" writes Schoek, "or the ubiquitous fear of it, means that there is little possibility of individual economic achieve-

---

6. Helmut Schoeck, *Envy: A Theory of Social Behavior* (New York: Harcourt, Brace & World, 1969), p. 37.

7. *Ibid.*, p. 40.

ment and no contact with the outside world through which the community might hope to progress. No one dares to show anything that might lead people to think he was better off. Innovations are unlikely. Agricultural methods remain traditional and primitive, to the detriment of the whole village, because every deviation from previous practice comes up against the limitations of envy."[8]

Furthermore, he continues, "It is impossible for several families to pool resources or tools of any kind in a common undertaking. It is almost equally impossible for any one man to adopt a leading role in the interests of the village."[9] While Schoeck does not discuss it, the problem of institutionalized envy and magic for the establishment of democratic institutions in primitive cultures is almost overwhelming. Once a chief's link to authority is destroyed, who is to lead? If a man cannot point to his family's long tradition or to his own authority or semi-divine status as ruler, who is to say who should lead? Whoever does proclaim himself as leader had better be prepared to defend his title from envy and magic. In a culture in which the authority of traditional rulers has been eroded by Western secularism and Western theories of individualism and democracy, the obvious alternative is *power*.

Perhaps most important as a retarding factor is the effect that envy has on men's concept of *time*. "In a culture incapable of any form of competition, time means nothing."[10] Men do not discuss their plans with each other. Shared goals, except of a traditional nature, are almost absent in magical societies. "Ubiquitous envy, fear of it and those who harbour it, cuts off such people from any kind of communal action directed towards the future. Every man is for himself, every man is thrown back upon his own resources. All striving, preparation and planning for the future can be undertaken only by socially fragmented, secretive beings."[11] Is it any wonder, then, that primitive cultures stay primitive, despite massive doses of foreign aid — state-to-state aid? Schoeck does not exaggerate when he concludes that as a system of social control, "Black Magic is of tremendous importance, because it governs all interpersonal relationships."[12]

---

8. *Ibid.*, p. 47.
9. *Ibid.*, p. 48.
10. *Ibid.*, p. 41.
11. *Ibid.*, p. 50.
12. *Ibid.*, p. 52.

The Conditions for Growth

The concept of general economic growth was not present in the pagan cultures of antiquity. It was only in Judaism and Christianity that such a view of life could flourish, precisely because economic growth was understood personally and culturally: it is the product of outward response to basic ethical requirements. Magical manipulation of the environment was rejected officially as an illegitimate form of economic practice. Prayer to a personal Creator by the humble believer is legitimate; ritual offerings to polytheistic deities of impersonal forces was outlawed. It is not ritual accuracy that God requires, but a humble heart and obedience to ethical laws (Micah 6:6-8). Christianity and Judaism prohibited envy and jealousy. Men are not to covet their neighbor's goods (Exodus 20:17), nor are they to envy the prosperity of the wicked (Proverbs 24:19-20).

The most comprehensive of all colonial American Puritan treatises was Rev. Samuel Willard's *Compleat Body of Divinity*, the largest book ever published in Puritan days (1726). It was a compilation of Willard's sermons on the Larger Catechism, which took him twenty years of Sunday evening services to finish. The section on the Eighth Commandment, which prohibits theft, contained a comprehensive critique on envy. Willard denied that we are hurt by our neighbor's advantages. (This fallacy has been called by Mises the *Montaigne dogma*, i.e., the belief that in an exchange of goods, one man's gain is the other's loss. It was a basic error of economic mercantilism, which was a prominent philosophy in Willard's day. Mises correctly argues that this doctrine is at the bottom of all modern theories of class conflict.)[13] Envy, Willard continued, feeds on greed. It leads to mischief. It is utterly unreasonable hate without a cause. It is an affront to God, for God has set men up for His purposes; envy is an affront to God's purposes and glory in this world. Furthermore, it despises God's gifts. It leads to covetousness (jealousy, in Schoeck's use of the term). Men should not be tempted to take revenge on those who are more prosperous than they are.[14] With preaching like this, men found it difficult to envy or covet openly their neighbor's prosperity. The fruits of men's personal labor could be safely displayed. It would pay men individually to plan for the future, both individually and in

13. Ludwig von Mises, *Human Action* (3rd ed.: Chicago: Regnery, 1966), p. 664.
14. Samuel Willard, *A Compleat Body of Divinity* (New York: Johnson Reprints, [1726] 1969), pp. 750-52.

groups. The free market could flourish because the ethical supports so fundamental for its existence were provided by Christian preaching and laws against magic.

Back to Magic?

Magic again is coming back into the thinking of Western men. By abandoning the belief in a Creator God and a world of personal law, modern man has been thrown back into the grim polarity of the classical world: blind impersonal fate vs. blind impersonal chance.[15] R. C. Zaehner is quite correct in beginning his study, *Zen, Drugs and Mysticism* (1972), with an analysis of the philosophy of the biologist, Jacques Monod (*Chance and Necessity*). Man is alone in an infinite world, simultaneously determined by and subject to total randomness. This is all the promise of science holds for man: an endless, meaningless process of determinism and indeterminism. Men seek to escape this world by means of *mystical illumination* (meditation, drugs, alpha-wave machines) or by means of *power from below* (magic and revolution). A world without God is a world without meaning. It is a world ripe for the satanic religion of magic.

From an economic point of view, we already have a widespread philosophy of envy present in industrial societies. If magic is reintroduced to the West, then cultural degeneration is assured. Modern society is not some autonomous mechanism. It needs ethical and philosophical support. We should heed Schoeck's warning: "The primitive people's belief in black magic differs little from modern ideas. Whereas the socialist believes himself robbed by the employer, just as the politician in a developing country believes himself robbed by the industrial countries, so primitive man believes himself robbed by his neighbor, the latter having succeeded by black magic in spiriting away to his own fields part of the former's harvest."[16] Modern secularism and socialism threaten us with economic reversal—the kind of disastrous reversal promised by God in the 28th chapter of Deuteronomy. Magic and envy, whether secular or animalistic, are equally primitive.

---

15. Charles Norris Cochrane, *Christianity and Classical Culture* (New York: Oxford University Press, [1940]), pp. 156-60.

16. Schoeck, *Envy*, p. 41.

2

UPPER-CLASS INVESTING

The concept of class position has been a dominant theme among scholars since the 19th century. Karl Marx founded communism in terms of a theory of history which asserted that class struggles underlie all historical development. But what, precisely, is a class? Marx never really said. In the third paragraph from the end of his posthumously published third volume of *Das Kapital*—which he never completed, although the main draft was completed about 15 years before he died—he wrote: "The first question to be answered is this: What constitutes a class?" Quite so; unfortunately for theoretical Marxism, he never was able to figure out an answer. But that hasn't stopped his followers from trying to take over the world in the name of the class struggle. Over a decade ago, Prof. Edward Banfield, the Harvard political scientist, offered a new definition of class. So unpopular was the book in which he offered his thesis that the students harassed him out of his job. He went to the University of Pennsylvania for a few years until things cooled off at Harvard. Then he went back. (It had been almost as bad at Pennsylvania. He actually required police protection at one stage.)

Banfield's thesis makes a great deal of sense. He defines class position in terms of time perspective, not income.

In the analysis to come, the individual's orientation toward the future will be regarded as a function of two factors: (1) ability to imagine a future, and (2) ability to discipline oneself to sacrifice present for future satisfaction. The more distant the future the individual can imagine and can discipline himself to make sacrifices for, the "higher" his class. The criterion, it should be noted, is ability, not performance . . . It must again be strongly emphasized that this use of the term "class" is different from the ordinary one. As the term is used here, a person who is poor, unschooled, and of low status may be upper-class; indeed he is upper-class if he is psychologically capable of providing for a distant future. By the same token, one who is

9

rich and a member of "the 400" may be lower class; he is lower-class if he is incapable of conceptualizing the future or of controlling his impulses and is therefore obliged to live from moment to moment. (*The Unheavenly City* [Boston: Little Brown, 1970], pp. 47-48.)

When we consider the ramifications of this definition of class for contemporary attitudes, the implications are grim. What we are seeing in the United States today is the steady increase of lower-class citizens. As men's time perspectives shift to the short run, their class position drops.

What made Banfield's detractors so furious was his argument that since class is a product of time perspective, the government is unlikely to be able to raise people in the ghetto to middle-class status. The government can pour billions of dollars into the ghettos, but the results will be very different from what the bureaucrats have promised. Without a lengthening of time perspective, without an increased commitment to deferred gratification, without an increase of self-discipline for future gains, the ghetto will remain pretty much what it is today.

The Lower Class. At the present-oriented end of the scale, the lower-class individual lives from moment to moment. If he has any awareness of the future, it is of something fixed, fates, beyond his control: things happen to him, he does not make them happen. Impulse governs his behavior, either because he cannot discipline himself to sacrifice a present for a future or because he has no sense of the future. He is therefore radically improvident: whatever he cannot consume immediately he considers valueless. His bodily needs (especially for sex) and his taste for "action" take precedence over everything else—and certainly over any work routine. He works only as he must to stay alive, and drifts from one unskilled job to another, taking no interest in the work (p. 53).

One of the finest examples in history of the difference between the two perspectives—long run vs. short run—is the exchange that took place between Jacob and Esau, the sons of Isaac. The Bible records that exchange. Esau came to Jacob claiming to be on the verge of starvation—a lie, by the way, since as soon as he was fed, he got up and walked away. Jacob demanded for a bowl of pottage something Esau possessed by law as the elder twin: the birthright. The birthright involved a double portion of the father's inheritance, but it also involved increased responsibility on the part of the oldest son for the care of the parents in their old age. Esau willingly traded his birthright for the immediate gratification of eating some stew (Genesis 25:29-34). Esau received exactly what he wanted: stew. Jacob received what he wanted: the birthright. Esau was intensely present-oriented. He put such a low value on the future, that he was willing to forego the special blessing of the birthright to fill up his stomach. Esau, the action-oriented hunter, was no match for Jacob, the drab fellow with a vision of the future.

Interest Rates

The existence of positive rates of interest stems from the distinction in the minds of men between now and later. Men make decisions constantly, choosing to do one thing and not another at any point in time. With the economists' assumption of "other things being equal," men would rather enjoy the use of a good or service in the present than in the future. Give a man the opportunity to choose between a free gift today or a year from now, and he will select today's gift. Therefore, men discount the value of future goods. They want to be compensated for their forfeiting the use of money now. This discount of future goods against present goods is the pure rate of interest, or original rate of interest. The higher men value the present in comparison to future goods, the higher the rate of interest they will pay to buy today's goods (and the higher the rate of interest they will demand in order to get them to part with their money now).

This provides us with important information concerning economic underdevelopment. If a large number of citizens are present-oriented, there will not be much economic growth in the society. After all, men get what they pay for. They want instant gratification, so they forfeit higher productivity (and higher income) in the future. They buy what they want. A present-oriented society will be marked by high rates of interest, and therefore lower rates of investment. Only very high profit opportunities will lure entrepreneurs into investment avenues. If you have to pay, say, 50% per annum interest rate or more, then you have to expect better than a 50% return on your money in order to get you to pull your money out of new cars, or out of money-lending, and into the creation of buying a new business. In effect, the present-oriented society is buying its higher level of present consumption by sacrificing economic growth in the future.

Conversely, societies that have a commitment to the future also tend to have low rates of interest. People don't charge a high premium in order to get them to part with their present capital. They want economic growth, and by forfeiting present consumption in order to buy economic growth, they attain their objectives.

The transformation of modern American culture into a present-oriented society has been going on for two generations or more—possibly since the Roaring Twenties. What we have seen is an increasing unwillingness of Americans to lend money, invest, and build for the future. Our savings rate today is under 4%, the lowest in American history and either the lowest or second lowest among Western industrial states. The present-orientation of all classes of society is pronounced. Men want instant gratification. Of course, prices being the same, future vs. present goods, we all want instant gratification. But prices are not the same. There is an interest rate, and it is predictable that it will get higher in the long run if this present-orientation continues to spread throughout society.

The rise of the drug culture, the advent of marijuana as a middle-money ("class") and even upper-money ("class") drug, the emphasis on leisure, and the youth culture all emphasize the value of present experiences over future experiences. The philosophy of "eat, drink, and be merry, for tomorrow we die" is calculated to raise interest rates and reduce investment, thereby stifling future economic growth.

Consider the implications of such a scenario for long-term bonds and mortgages. Rising rates will begin to squeeze out the poorer and middle-money ("class") purchasers of homes. Without bond financing, new uncertainties will be placed on economic development. The pay-off period for investments will get shorter, which means that long-term investing will become more difficult, more costly. The availability of lendable funds at anything like historic rates of interest will dry up. Entrepreneurs will be forced to go with higher risk investments, in order to get the necessary pay-off fast enough to pay the loans.

This will mean disaster for real estate development, unless the Federal government steps in to make below-market loans available. But if the government does this—and it's almost a sure thing—then the Federal deficit will get larger, and more fiat money will have to be injected into the system. But fiat money raises prices, and rising prices raises long-term interest rates, since lenders tack on an "inflation premium" to loans, in order to compensate themselves for the fall in the dollar's purchasing power. To keep the real estate markets alive, and to keep savings & loan associations solvent, the government will have to continue the mad race between fiat money and long-term interest rates, with the dollar-denominated price of housing continuing to soar, right alongside of mortgage rates.

Keynes' Legacy

John Maynard Keynes defended the short-run applications of his inflationary economic policies by remarking, "In the long run, we are all dead." So are paper currencies. Keynes' remark typifies twentieth-century interventionist economics: a short-run perspective that justifies the hampering of the market—the source of long-run growth in output and wealth.

Obviously, there are exceptions to the spread of short-run thinking. But on the whole, it does describe what's happening to America. Inflation is making people think in short-run terms. Men face increasingly erratic markets, wider swings in the boom-bust cycles, and the threat of monetary breakdown. They shift their focus from 20-year projects to 5-year projects. They have to. Nobody can calculate the economic future 20 years down the road. The best guesses become an amusing intellectual exercise. The next wave of inflation will wipe out holders of long-term, dollar-denominated assets. Already, they are being hurt badly. The long-term capital markets are being threatened by a combination of inflation and present-oriented consumers. This is Keynes' legacy: more aggregate demand, more consumer spending, more personal and government debt, less savings. This was Keynes' program for economic reconstruction. The bills are coming due.

A friend of mine visited Argentina in 1979. He reported that there was a lot of economic activity, but that the capital base shows the effects of decades of price inflation. Homes of the rich are stately, but they are running down. Plumbing is old, sometimes half a century out of date. The rich are consuming the capital of their parents and grandparents. The replacement costs of capital have soared, as a result of unanticipated price inflation.

We can expect to face serious inflation over the next decade. The government will continue to make available below-market loans to favored industries and voting groups. We should therefore begin taking seriously Keynes' dictum that in the long run, we are all dead. But in the intermediate run, we are mostly alive, but without capital. The inflation wipes out our capital base before many of us reach retirement age. And for those who have reached retirement age, the government is about to produce a nightmare. This is why sensible investors are rethinking all the traditional avenues of investment. They have to hedge against the coming inflation.

The Grandfather Factor

The President of Grove City College, a 4-year liberal arts college in Northwest Pennsylvania, remarked to me that his college decided several years ago to make large investments in plant facilities. Grove City College is that rarity, a debt-free private college. Instead of building new athletic facilities, or using the money to expand student enrollment, the trustees decided to upgrade the school's physical plant. "In the future," he told me, "we know we may be caught in a financial squeeze because of the inflation. We want to be able to coast later on, without bleeding the college dry by having to make expensive capital repairs."

This is a very sensible philosophy today. I cannot recommend it highly enough. If you are satisfied with your geographical location — safety, future potential, etc. — then I would strongly recommend upgrading your home. I would recommend that real estate speculators now start putting more money into improving the value of their properties, rather than continuing to pyramid them. If the experience of Argentina's rich is any guide, we can expect to face a lengthy period of capital erosion. We can also expect to experience the "invisible inflation" of reduced quality. Manufacturers will adjust their perspective to meet the time demands of the public. If the public is buying instant, cost-effective gratification, then quality considerations will begin to fall by the wayside.

This reduction in product quality is not universal. Some products maintain their markets by means of a reputation for quality. But these products are generally aimed at the upper classes: the rich, or more precisely, those who can afford and who understand the value of durable goods. The "eat, drink, and be merry" outlook is inimical to upper-class time perspectives. The "throw-away society" is not the product of long-term perspectives.

The perspective of the grandfather is at the heart of this investment strategy. If a man's philosophy is that of the Schlitz commercial, "You only go around once in life, so grab all the gusto you can " then his attitude toward his grandchildren will be very different from that most familiar in Europe, where the preservation of family capital and the family name is basic to economic decisions, or was a generation ago. The story of Johnny Appleseed is representative of men's long-term planning. We have to look beyond our own life-spans.

Again, this is another area in which the Federal government's policies are wiping out this nation. There is no worse tax than the inheritance tax. It tells men, "Use up your capital today. Don't look ahead beyond the grave. You can't control what your kids do. Forget about leaving them a pile of capital. Just live it up now, and to encourage you in this, the Federal government and state governments will see to it that you can't leave that much." This shortens the time perspective of men.

For example, men set up trusts for children at early ages because of the gift tax consequences of delaying the decision. But sometimes they wind up with too much money at an early age. So we look for ways to train them. One of the best ways is to use trust assets to buy income-producing real estate. The child is told from an early age that this will be his asset, that he must make the best of it that he can. He has to mange it, fix it up, hire the repairmen, keep the books, pay the taxes, and generally get himself involved in entrepreneurship, or at least basic management. But how many trustees ever think of such a strategy? Not many.

The idea that capital can be built up and passed down, generation after generation, with the potential always present of expanding it, and expanding the influence of those who bear the family name, has been seriously compromised by modern estate tax laws. We have substituted the State as the eldest son. It gets the double portion, and it becomes legally responsible for the care of the parents. But this child is a parasite. It never grows up. It never learns to be productive. It absorbs, steals, and redistributes. The result: the creation of a pseudo-family, a true monster. We have sold our children's birthright to the State for a mess of pottage (or, more to the point, a socialistic pot of message).

Our proper goal is to train up children who are truly upper-class. They have a commitment to the future. They have an understanding that their efforts have long-term consequences. We must strive to create a moral perspective in our children's minds that offsets the siren call of the short run in our day. Ultimately, I know of no capital investment more important than this—not gold, not diamonds, not AAA bonds.

This having been done to the best of our ability, then we must adopt a strategy of wealth-transfer. We have to be realistic about the future. We are going to see the shaking of the economic foundations in the West over the next decade. I think we may see the destruction of the dollar. This being a distinct possibility, we then face some sort of revolutionary transformation: the coming of socialism, or fascism, or a major economic depression, or perhaps a return to the free market. What you must do is to transfer wealth, or claims to wealth, to the next generation in ways not easy to trace. Also, we need to put their visible assets in forms that will probably withstand the ravages of inflation, price controls, and even a full-scale redistributionist State.

Records

My continual suggestion to people who are trying to make long-run investments is this: with the exception of real estate (where the voters are on your side), don't leave a trail of paper. Train up children in the knowledge of alternative markets. If a child has a hobby, encourage it. After all, if your parents had encouraged you to collect electric trains as a kid, you would be worth a bundle today. The point I'm trying to make is simple enough: educate your children for the world which is probably coming, and coming very soon. I like family businesses for this reason. But the more the business is capable of operating underground, if not now then in the future, the better it is for training purposes. The training will survive, even if the capital does get confiscated at some point.

Over and over, I stress the importance of goods, not paper. Put your capital in durable goods, especially productive tools. Services are easier to swap without leaving a trail of paper. Get the tools now, so that you will be ready for swapping later. The investment should be regarded as a means of purchasing future invisibility.

The long-run perspective takes discipline. People want a fast pay-off. They want visible confirmation of their genius, measurable in dollars and cents, and easily displayed to the brother-in-law. This is what keeps so many people in the conventional markets. They are not after long-run gains, meaning lifetime gains. They are after brilliant tips that will reflect their own genius.

It is a lot more difficult than you think to break the habits of short-run, or lower-class investing. The guy who buys a gold coin, watches its dollar-denominated price rise, and then brags to his friends about this success, hasn't understood the nature of the economic and political problem. While most gold coin investors are less likely to play this game, I know South African gold share people who are caught up in this "displayable genius" approach.

The longer term you're considering, the quieter the investment should be. The fewer records it should leave, because the political transformation of the next decade will shock millions of those who have invested in terms of "business as usual."

I am partial to numismatic (rare) coins because of their long-term potential. The longer you wait to sell, the more you have time on your side. Coins get rarer, and their prices climb. I think that they are very good in trust funds for younger children — matched by real estate as they grow more responsible. I think they are right for personal and professional corporation retirement funds. But remember, these are paper money investments, ultimately. You will trade them in for paper eventually. The idea is to structure your "hard goods" investments to get time working for you, and rare items have this advantage. In a major collapse, they are not the best asset, but on the far side of a collapse, they should perform very well. They are also easier to move rapidly in a crisis.

I think the tax laws will be changed several times over the next decade or two. I think there is a reason why the Federal government has encouraged proliferation of retirement programs for little people and directors of professional (one-man) corporations. I think the reason has something to do with getting people's assets far more visible. Visible assets are the best kind from the perspective of the tax collector.

What you need is a sizable proportion of your assets held in forms that can withstand sharp discontinuities, especially tax laws. You don't need to see your capital go up with every inflationary boom. It may even sometimes sag with the temporary drops in the economy. What you need to do is to concentrate on those assets that hold up well over long periods of time. The simplest is small gold coins. Close behind is silver. You can "buy and forget," which is what you need if you're to devote the bulk of your time to your profession.

The longer your time frame, the better off you will be. The short run must be dealt with on a regular basis, but decisions concerning the long run can be made now with the lowest cost.

What whipsaws out well-meaning investors is the action of the markets, the 6-month movements that seem to indicate that the basic direction of the economy is not toward mass inflation, higher taxes, and controls. But we live in an age of short-term perspectives, both economic and political. For survival, we have to aim beyond the targets announced in *Newsweek*. For survival, we need to discipline ourselves to become upper-class investors.

3

THE MORAL ISSUE OF "HONEST MONEY"

Because of the nature of the economics profession — "guild" might be a better word — it is necessary to put quotation marks around the words, "honest money." Economists will go to almost any length to avoid the use of moral terms when they discuss economic issues. This has been true since the seventeenth century, when early mercantilistic pamphlet writers tried to avoid religious controversy by creating the illusion of moral and religious neutrality in their writings. This, they falsely imagined, would produce universal agreement, or at least more readily debatable disagreements, since "scientific" arguments are open to rational investigation. The history of both modern science and modern economics since the seventeenth century has demonstrated how thoroughly unreconcilable the scientists are, morality or no morality.

Nevertheless, traditions die hard. Economists are not supposed to inject questions of morality into their analysis. Economics is still supposedly a "positive" science, one concerned strictly with questions of "if. . . . then." If the government does A, then B is likely to result. If the government wants to achieve D, then it should adopt policy E. The economist can therefore deal with "complete neutrality" with this sort of problem: "If the Nazis wish to exterminate 50,000 people, which are the most cost-effective means?" No morality, you understand, just simple economic analysis.

The problem with the theory of neutral economics is that people are not neutral, effects of government policies are not neutral, social systems are not neutral, legal systems are not neutral, and when pressed, even economists are not neutral. Because societies are not neutral, the costs of violating a society's first principles have to be taken into account. But no economist can do any more than guess about such costs. There is no known way to assess the true costs to society of having its political leaders defy fundamental moral prin-

ciples in adopting any given policy. And if the economists guess wrong
— not an unlikely prospect, given the hypothetical moral vacuum in
which economists officially operate — then the whole society will pay.
(This assumes, of course, that policy-makers listen to economists.)

The inability of economists to make accurate cost-benefit analyses
of any and all policy matters is a kind of skeleton in the profession's
closet. The problem was debated back in the late 1930s, and a few
economists still admit that it is a real theoretical problem, but very few
think about it. The fact of the matter is simple: there is no measuring
device for balancing total individual utility vs. total disutility for society as a whole. You cannot, as a scientist, make interpersonal comparisons of subjective utility. The better economists know this, but they
prefer not to think about it. They want to give advice, but as scientists
they cannot say what policy is better for society as a whole.[1]

This is why politicians and policy-makers have to rely on intui-
tion, just as the economists do. There is no scientific standard to tell
them whether or not a particular policy should be imposed. Without
a concept of morality — that some policy is morally superior to another
— the economists' "if. . . . then" game will not answer the questions
that need to be answered. Without moral guidelines, there is little
hope of guessing correctly the true costs and benefits to society as a
whole of any policy. The economist, as a scientist, is in no better
position to make such estimations than anyone else. If anything, he
is in a worse position, since his academic training has conditioned
him to avoid mixing moral issues and economic analysis. He is not
used to dealing with such questions.

What Is Honest Money?

Honest money is a social institution that arises from honest deal-
ings among acting individuals. Money is probably best defined as
the most marketable commodity. I accept a dollar in exchange for

---

1. For those who are curious about this great debate over the impossibility of
making interpersonal comparisons of subjective utility, see the exchange that took
place between Sir Roy Harrod and Lionel Robbins: Roy F. Harrod, "Scope and
Methods of Economics," *The Economic Journal*, (Sept., 1938) and Lionel Robbins,
"Interpersonal Comparisons of Utility: A Comment," *The Economic Journal* (Dec.,
1938). For some "new left" conclusions concerning the results of this debate, see
Mark A. Lutz and Kenneth Lux, *The Challenge of Humanistic Economics* (Menlo Park,
Calif.: Benjamin/Cummings, 1979), pp. 83-89. For my own observations on its im-
plications, see Gary North, *The Dominion Covenant: Genesis* (Tyler, Texas: Institute for
Christian Economics, 1982), ch. 4.

goods or services that I supply only because I have reason to suspect that someone else will do the same for me later on. If I begin to suspect that others will refuse to take my dollar in exchange for their goods and services in the future, I will be less willing to take that dollar today. I may ask the buyer to pay me a dollar and a quarter, just to compensate me for my risk in holding that dollar over time.

A currency unit functions as money—a medium of voluntary exchange—only because people expect it to do so in the future. One reason why they expect a particular currency unit to be acceptable in the future is that it has been acceptable in the past. A monetary unit has to have historic value in most instances if it is to function as money. Occasionally, meaning very rarely, a government can impose a new currency unit on its citizens, and sometimes this works. One good example is the introduction of the new German mark in November of 1923, which was exchanged for the old mark at a trillion to one. But normally the costs are so high in having people rethink and relearn a new currency unit that governments avoid such an imposition.

Historic Stability

The question policy-makers must ask themselves is this: To avoid the necessity of imposing a totally new currency unit on a population, what can be done to convince people that the future usefulness of the currency in voluntary exchange will remain high? What can be done to improve the historic value of money in the future? In other words, when people in a year or a decade look back at the performance of their nation's currency unit, will they say to themselves: "This dollar that I'm holding today buys pretty much what it bought back then. I think it's safe for me to continue to accept dollars in exchange for my goods and services, since people trust its buying power. I have no reason to believe that its purchasing power will fall in the future, so I can take the risk of accepting payment in dollars today." If people do not say this to themselves, then the dollar's purchasing power is undermined. People will demand more dollars in payment, meaning prices will go up, if they suspect that prices will go up. This, in turn, convinces more people that the historic value of their money has been unreliable, which then leads to higher prices.

The economist will tell you that prices cannot continue to go up unless the government, working with the central bank, accommodates price inflation by expanding the currency base. The economist is correct in the long run, whatever the long run is these days, or will be in a few years. But governments have a pernicious tendency to accommodate price inflation. Dr. Arthur Burns was forthright about this back in 1976:

> These days the Federal Reserve is now and then described as pursuing a restrictive monetary policy. The Federal Reserve is described as being engaged in a struggle against inflation. The Federal Reserve is even charged with being more concerned about inflation than about unemployment, which is entirely false. It is by generating inflation, or permitting inflation, that we get unemployment on a massive scale eventually. But let us ask the Federal Reserve this question: Are we accommodating inflation at the present time or not? The answer—the only honest, professional answer—is that, to a large degree, we are accommodating the inflation; in other words, are making it possible for inflation to continue.[2]

So we get a kind of self-fulfilling prophecy. The government expands the money supply in order to finance its deficits, or create a temporary economic boom, or whatever, and the prices for goods and services rise. Everyone in the "great American auction" has more dollars to use in the bidding process, so prices rise. Then the public gets suspicious about the future value of money, because they have seen the loss of purchasing power in the past. They demand higher prices. Then the Federal Reserve System is encouraged by politicians to accommodate the price inflation, in order to keep the boom going (to keep the "auction" lively). The dollar loses its present value, because it has lost its historic value, which encourages people to discount sharply its future value.

The secret of retaining the public's confidence in any currency unit is simple enough: convince users of the money that the issuers are responsible, reliable, and trustworthy. Government and its licensed agents have a monopoly of money creation. Private competitors are called counterfeiters. Sadly, in our day, it is very difficult to understand just what it is that counterfeiters do, economically speaking, that governments are not already doing. Fiat money is fiat money. (Perhaps the real legal issue ought to be the illegal use of the government's copyrighted material. Copyright infringement makes a

---

2. *Federal Reserve Consultations on the Conduct of Monetary Policy*, Hearings Before the Committee on Banking, Currency and Housing, House of Representatives, 94th Congress, 2nd Session (July 27 and 28, 1976), pp. 26-27. Printed by the U.S. Government Printing Office, Washington, D.C.

much more logical case for Federal prosecution than counterfeiting.)

Who Guards the Guardians?

There is an ancient question that every society must answer: "Who guards the guardians?" Or in more contemporary usage, "Who referees the referees?" The public needs an impersonal guardian to restrain the actions of those who hold a legal monopoly of money creation: the government, the central bank, and the commercial banks. The public can guard the guardians if citizens have the right to go down to the local bank and receive payment in gold, silver, or some other money metal. The issuers of money need only stamp on the paper money (or check, or deposit book entry) that the holder of the currency unit has a legal right to redeem his warehouse receipt for a stated weight and fineness of a specific metal.[3] Whenever the issuing agencies begin to issue more receipts than they have reserves of metal, the public has the option of "calling the bluff" of the issuers, and demanding payment, as promised by law. It is this restraint—implicit economically, but explicit legally—which serves as the impersonal guardian of the public trust.

The government can always change the law. Governments do this all the time. Whenever there is a major war, for example, governments suspend specie payments. They also suspend civil liberties, and for the same reason: to increase the power of the state at the expense of the citizens. Governments in peacetime are frequently unwilling to reestablish pre-war taxes, pre-war civil liberties, and pre-war convertibility of currencies, long after the war is over. Civil libertarians have not generally understood the case for a gold standard as a case for civil liberties, despite the obvious historical correlation between wartime suspension of civil liberties and wartime suspension of specie payments.

When the authorities declare the convertibility of paper into specie metals "null and void," it sends the public a message. "Attention! This is your government speaking. We are no longer willing to subject ourselves to your continual interference in our governmental affairs. We no longer can tolerate illegitimate restrictions on our efforts to guard the public welfare, especially from the public. Therefore, we are suspending the following civil right: the public's legal

---

3. On money as a warehouse receipt, see Murray N. Rothbard, *Man, Economy and State* (New York: New York University Press, [1962] 1975), pp. 700-3.

right to call our bluff when we guarantee free convertibility of our currency. This should not be interpreted as an immoral act on the part of the government. Contracts are not moral issues. They are strictly pragmatic. However, we assure you, from the bottom of our collective heart, that we shall never expand the money supply, or allow the historic value of the currency to depreciate. It will be just as if we had a gold standard restraint on our printing presses. However, such restraints are unnecessary, and besides, they are altogether too restraining."

Redeemability Required

Critics of the gold standard tell us that the value of any currency is dependent on public confidence, not gold. But what the critics refuse to admit is that the existence of the civil liberty of redeemable money is an important psychological support of the public's confidence in money. Even when the public does not understand the gold standard's theoretical justification—an impersonal guard of the monopolistic guardians—citizens can exercise their judgment on a daily basis by either demanding payment in gold (or silver, or whatever) or not demanding payment. Like the free market itself, it works whether or not the bulk of the participants understand the theory. What they do understand is self-interest: if there is a profit to be made from buying gold at the official rate, and selling it into the free market (including foreign markets) at a higher price, then some people will enter the markets as middlemen, "buying low and selling high," until the government realizes that its bluff has been called, and it therefore is forced to reduce the expansion of the money supply.

What is the morality of a gold standard? Simple: it is the morality of a legal contract. A government's word is its bond. A government promises to restrain itself in the creation of money, in order to assure citizens that the monopoly of money-creation will not be abused by those holding the monopoly grant of power. The gold standard is very much like a constitution: an impersonal, reliable institution which has as its premier function the counterbalancing of potentially damaging monopolistic power.

"Flexible" Money

Flexible money is a euphemism for the government's ability to increase (but, historically speaking, rarely to decrease) the money supply. The degree of flexibility is determined by the political process, not by the direct response of those affected, namely, individual citizens who would otherwise have the right to demand payment in gold. Flexible money means monetary inflation. Very flexible money means a whole lot of monetary inflation. Monetary inflation means, within 24 months, price inflation.

Civil libertarians instantly recognize the danger of "flexible censorship," or "flexible enforcement of speed traps." Yet they have great difficulty in recognizing precisely the same kind of evil in "flexible monetary policy." The threat comes from the same institution, the civil government. It comes for the same reasons: the desire of the government to increase its arbitrary exercise of monopolistic power over the citizenry and to limit public resistance.

The inflationary implications of "flexible monetary policy" can be seen in a revealing exchange between Arthur Burns and Henry Reuss:

> DR. BURNS: Let me say this, if I may: the genius of monetary policy — its great virtue — is that it is flexible. With respect to the growth ranges that we project for the coming year, as I have tried to advise this committee from time to time — and as I keep reminding others, including members of my own Federal Reserve family — our goal at the Federal Reserve is not to make a particular projection come true; our goal is to adjust what we do with a view to achieving a good performance of the economy. If at some future time I should come to this committee and report a wide discrepancy between our projection and what actually happened in the sphere of money and credit, I would not be embarrassed in the slightest. On the contrary, I would feel that the Federal Reserve had done well and I would even anticipate a possible word of praise from this generous committee.
>
> CHAIRMAN REUSS: You would get it, and the word of praise would be even louder and more deeply felt if you came up and said that due to the change in circumstances you were proving once again that you were not locked on automatic pilot and were willing to become more expansive if the circumstances warranted. Either way you would get praise beyond belief.[4]

Praise beyond belief! Who wants anything less? Just take the monetary system off "automatic pilot," and turn it over to those whose short-run political goals favor a return of the inflation-generated economic boom, once the boom has worn off because the printing presses are not accelerating the output of fiat money — fiat money being defined as former warehouse receipts for metal, in which even

---

4. *Federal Reserve Consultations*, p. 13.

the pretense of a warehouse has been abandoned. Gold is a tough-minded automatic pilot.

Politically, there is a great deal of flexibility in monetary affairs. Few people even pretend to understand monetary affairs, and most of those who do really do not understand the logic of the gold standard. The logic is very simple, very clear, and universally despised: it is cheaper to print money than it is to dig gold.

Problems with Fiat Money

Fiat money is indeed more flexible than gold, especially in an upward direction. Fiat money allows the government to spend newly manufactured money into circulation. It allows those who gain early access to the newly created fiat money to go out and buy up scarce economic resources at yesterday's prices — prices based on supply and demand conditions that were being bid in terms of yesterday's money supply. But this leads to some important problems.

1. Yesterday's prices will climb upward to adjust for today's money supply.

2. People will begin to have doubts about the stability of tomorrow's prices.

3. Producers and sellers of resources may begin to discount the future purchasing power of today's dollar (that is, hike today's prices in anticipation).

4. The government or central bank will be severely tempted to "accommodate" rising prices by expanding the money supply.

5. And the beat goes on.

Paying for the Guards

It is quite true, as Milton Friedman has stated so graphically, that the gold standard is expensive.[5] We dig gold out of the ground in one location, only to bury it in the ground in another location. We cannot do this for free. Wouldn't it be more efficient, meaning less wasteful of scarce economic resources, Dr. Friedman asks, just to forget about digging up gold? Why not keep the government or the central bank from expanding the money supply? Then the same

---

5. Writes Prof. Friedman: "My conclusion is that an automatic commodity standard is neither a feasible nor a desirable solution to the problem of establishing monetary arrangements for a free society. It is not desirable because it would involve a large cost in the form of resources used to produce the monetary commodity." *Capitalism and Freedom* (Chicago: University of Chicago Press, 1962), p. 42.

ends could be accomplished so much less wastefully. Save resources: trust politicians.

This is a very strange argument, coming as it does from a man who understands the efficiency of market processes, as compared to political and bureaucratic processes. The gold standard is the way that individual citizens, acting to increase their own personal advantage, can profit from any monetary inflation on the part of the monetary authorities. They can "buy low and sell high" simply by exchanging paper money for gold at the undervalued, official exchange rate, and hoarding gold in expectation of a higher price, or selling it into the free market at a higher price. Why is the price higher? Because individuals expect the government to go back on its promise, raise the official price of gold (that is, devalue the currency unit), or close the gold window altogether. Citizens can become future-predicting, risk-bearing, uncertainty-bearing speculators in a very restricted market, namely, the market for government promises. It allows those who are skeptical about the trustworthiness of government promises to take a profit-seeking position in the market. It allows those who trust the government to deposit money at 6 per cent or 10 per cent or whatever. Each side can speculate concerning the trustworthiness of government promises concerning redeemability of the currency, or more to the point, government promises concerning the future stability of the currency unit's purchasing power.

Let the Market Function

Defenders of the commodity futures markets—and this includes Dr. Friedman—argue that the existence of a market for future delivery and future payment of commodities smooths out market prices, since it opens the market to those who are willing to bear the uncertainties of predicting the future. Those who are successful predictors increase their profits, and therefore increase their strength in establishing market prices according to the true future conditions of supply and demand. Those who are less successful soon are forced out of the futures markets, thereby passing along capital to those who are more successful predictors. The public is served well by such markets, for obvious reasons. Prices adjust to future consumer demand more rapidly, since accurate future-predictors are being rewarded in these markets.

Then why not a market for future government promises? Why not a market which can test the government's willingness to deliver a stated quantity and fineness of gold or silver (but preferably gold, given international exchange)? The monopolists who control the money supply then are faced with a market which offers rewards to those who are willing and able to "call the monopolists' bluff" and demand gold for the government's warehouse receipts.

Why not just rely on the standard commodity contracts for gold in the commodity futures markets? Won't skeptics be able to take their profits this way? Why bring in the "spurious" issue of a convertible currency? The answer is simple enough: once society has given a monopoly to the government to create money, then the full redeemability of the currency unit is a direct, immediately felt restriction on government power. Of course the free market in commodities allows speculators to take advantage of monetary inflation, if their timing is correct. But this does not mean that the public at large will exercise effective action to force a political change in present monetary policy. There is no immediate self-interest involved in expending resources in what could prove to be a fruitless, expensive campaign to stop the inflation.

Fixing the Responsibility

In the commodities market, one investor wins, and one investor loses (unless the price stays the same, in which case only the broker wins). By establishing the gold standard—full redeemability of gold on public demand—the government forces the Treasury to risk becoming an immediate, measurable loser. It forces the Treasury's officials to come back to the politicians and announce, "Folks, we have lost the bet. The public has called our bluff. They have drained us of our gold. We can't go on much longer. We have to convince the public to start trusting the currency, meaning that they should start trusting our competence in securing them a currency with a future. We have to balance the budget. Stop inflating!"

An open commodities market in gold is desirable, of course. But it is no substitute for a gold standard if the state has a monopoly of money creation (along with its licensed subcontractors, the banks). Unless there is full redeemability, the Treasury is not forced by law to "go long" on its promises whenever anyone else wants to "go short."

Without full redeemability, the Treasury, meaning the government, can keep on shorting its own promises, despite the response of organized commodities markets, until an expensive and successful political campaign can be launched to stabilize the money supply. As free market analysis tells us, these campaigns are expensive to launch because of such factors as information costs, costs of organizing pressure groups, and the lack of an immediate, short-run pay-off to "investors" who contribute money to such a program. Full redeemability allows market forces to work. Self-interested forecasters can speculate in the government promises market. The public never has to be told to vote, send letters of protest, or do anything. The self-interested speculators—a small but well-capitalized elite—will do the "policing" job for the citizens free of charge.[6] (Well, almost: there are transaction costs.)

So when we are told that it is inefficient to dig gold out of the ground, only to deposit it in a vault, we are not being told the whole story. By tying the currency unit to that gold—which is wonderfully expensive to mine, as any monetary brake should be and must be— the body politic enlists a cadre of professional, self-interested speculators to serve as an unpaid police force. This police force polices the trustworthiness of government monetary promises. The public can relax, knowing that a hard core of greedy capitalists is at work for the public interest, monitoring Federal budgets, Federal Reserve policies, and similarly arcane topics. By forcing the Treasury to "go long" in its own promises market, the guardians are guarded by the best guards of all: future-predicting, self-interested speculators whose job it is to embarrass those who do not honor contracts— monetary contracts.

Conclusions

I suppose I could invest more time in presenting graphs, or faking some impressive-looking equations, or citing innumerable forgotten defenders of the gold standard. But I think I have reached the point of diminishing returns. The logic of the gold standard is really fairly simple: Treasury monopolists, like all other monopolists, cannot be trusted to honor their promises. Better put, they cannot be trusted at zero cost. The gold standard is one relatively inexpensive way to impose high costs on government monetary officials who do not honor their implicit contracts with the body politic to monitor

---

6. "By creating monitors with a vested interest in the maximization of a given set of values, property rights reduce the social cost of monitoring efficiency." Thomas Sowell, *Knowledge and Decisions* (New York: Basic Books, 1980), p. 125.

and deliver a reliable currency unit that will have future value—a trustworthy money system.

There are moral issues involved: honoring contracts, preserving social stability, providing a trustworthy government. There are civil liberties issues involved: protecting citizens from unwarranted taxation through monetary inflation, protecting citizens from arbitrary (read: "flexible") monetary policies, and restricting the expansion of government power. There are economic issues involved: designing an institutional mechanism that will bring self-interest to bear on political-economic policies, to stabilize purchasing power, to increase the spread of information in the community, and to increase the political risks for money monopolists. No doubt, I could go on, but these arguments seem sufficient.

The real question is more fundamental: Do we trust governments or the high costs of mining precious metals? William McChesney Martin, Dr. Burns' predecessor as Chairman of the Federal Reserve Board, gave us the options back in 1968, in the midst of an international monetary crisis: "It's governments that you have to rely on. Basically, you can't rely on a metal for solvency."[7]

Those of us who cannot bring ourselves to trust the government with any monopoly over the control of money prefer to trust a metal. It may not be the best thing to trust, but it is certainly more reliable than governments.

Keeping Government Honest

The case for a gold standard is the case against arbitrary civil government. While politicians may well resent "automatic pilots" in the sphere of monetary policy, if we had a more automatic pilot, we would have less intensive "boom-bust" cycles. When the "automatic pilot" is subject to tinkering by politicians or Federal Reserve officials, then it is not automatic any longer.

The appeal of specie metals is not the lure of magical talismans, as some critics of gold seem to imply. Gold is not a barbarous relic. Gold is a metal which, over millennia, has become acceptable as a means of payment in a highly complex institutional arrangement: the monetary system. Gold is part of civilization's most important economic institution, the division of labor-based monetary system.

---

7. William McChesney Martin, quoted in the *Los Angeles Times* (March 19, 1968), Pt. I, p. 12.

Without this division of labor, which monetary calculation has made possible, most of the world's population would be dead within a year, and probably within a few weeks. The alternative to the free market social order is government tyranny, some military-based centralized allocation system. Any attempt by the state to alter men's voluntary decisions in the area of exchange, including their choice of exchange units, represents the true relic of barbarism, namely, the use of force to determine the outcome of men's decisions.

The gold standard offers men an alternative to the fiat money systems that have transferred massive monopolistic power to the civil government. The gold standard is not to be understood as a restraint on men's freedom, but just the opposite: a means of restraining that great enemy of freedom, the arbitrary state. A gold standard restores an element of impersonal predictability to voluntary exchange — impersonal in the limited sense of not being subject to the whims of any individual or group. This predictability helps to reduce the uncertainties of life, and therefore helps to reduce the costs of human action. It is not a zero-cost institution, but it has proven itself as an important means of reducing arbitrary government. It is an "automatic pilot" which the high-flying, loud-crashing political daredevils resent. That, it seems to me, is a vote in its favor.

4

WALKING INTO A TRAP

There is some justification, at least, in the taunt that many of the pretending defenders of "free enterprise" are in fact defenders of privileges and advocates of government activity in their favor, rather than opponents of all privilege. In principle, the industrial protectionism and government-supported cartels and the agricultural policies of the conservative groups are not different from the proposals for a more far-reaching direction of economic life sponsored by the socialists. It is an illusion when the more conservative interventionists believe that they will be able to confine these government controls to the particular kinds of which they approve. In a democratic society, at any rate, once the principle is admitted that the government undertakes responsibility for the status and position of particular groups, it is inevitable that this control will be extended to satisfy the aspirations and prejudices of the great masses. There is no hope of a return to a freer system until the leaders of the movement against state control are prepared first to impose upon themselves that discipline of a competitive market which they ask the masses to accept.[1]

The idea that businessmen are strong defenders of the free enterprise system is one which is believed only by those who have never studied the history of private enterprise in the Western, industrial nations. What businessmen are paid to worry about is profit. The problem for the survival of a market economy arises when the voters permit or encourage the expansion of government power to such an extent that private businesses can gain short term profits through the intervention into the competitive market by state officials. Offer the typical businessman the opportunity to escape the constant pressures of market competition, and few of them are able to withstand the temptation. In fact, they are rewarded for taking the step of calling in the civil government.

---

1. F. A. Hayek, *Individualism and Economic Order* (University of Chicago Press, [1948] 1963), pp. 107-8. This is taken from Hayek's address to the Mont Pelerin Society in 1947.

The government's officials approve, but more to the point, from the point of view of the businessman's understanding of his role, shareholders and new investors also approve, since the favored enterprise is initially blessed with increased earnings per share. The business leader has his decision confirmed by the crucial standards of reference in the market, namely, rising profits and rising share prices on the stock market. No one pays the entrepreneur to be ideologically pure. Almost everyone pays him to turn a profit.

This being the case, those within the government possess an extremely potent device for expanding political power. By a comprehensive program of direct political intervention into the market, government officials can steadily reduce the opposition of businessmen to the transformation of the market into a bureaucratic, regulated, and even centrally-directed organization. Bureaucracy replaces entrepreneurship as the principal form of economic planning. Bureaucrats can use the time honored pair of motivational approaches: the carrot and the stick. The carrot is by far the most effective device when dealing with profit-seeking businessmen.

These individual enterprises that are expected to benefit from some new government program have every short-run financial incentive to promote the intervention, while those whose interests are likely to be affected adversely — rival firms, foreign enterprises, and especially consumers — find it expensive to organize their opposition, since the adverse effects are either not recognized as stemming from the particular government program, or else the potential opponents are scattered over too wide an area to be organized inexpensively. The efforts of the potential short-run beneficiaries are concentrated and immediately profitable; the efforts of the potential losers are dispersed and usually ineffective.

The expansion of political power in the market process has been going on in the West for about a century, at least in the modern form of interventionism, starting with the social security legislation of Bismarck's Germany in the 1870s. Governments have evolved a strategy by which whole industries or professions are captured by the bureaucratic state. While this strategy is not the only one used, in peacetime it has proven enormously successful. (Nothing, of course, favors political centralization more than war.) I have outlined this strategy by means of the following analogy:

1. Baiting the trap
2. Setting the trap
3. Springing the trap
4. Skinning the victim

Baiting the Trap—Extra Market Benefits

The politicians enter an otherwise competitive market situation with an offer to promote certain industrial or professional programs. Taxpayers' money is used to finance this program, but it is rare for the potential short-run beneficiaries to reject the offer on these grounds. Certainly, a majority of those who are to be the recipients of the special favor gladly accept it. They see their goals as being part of the public interest, and they view an offer of government aid as being only natural. They see it as their due. Those who refuse to take the special favor risk lower profits in the immediate future, since competitors in the industry or professional association will take the favor. The general attitude is this one: "If I don't take it, somebody else will." As a statement of fact, rather than principle, it is absolutely correct. Somebody else will.

There are several possible forms in which the aid may come. Industrial groups may receive *tariff protection*, which is a tax levied on consumers on both sides of a border over which trade had been carried on or over which it might be carried on in the future. Consumers pay higher prices on both sides. There can be no grants of government economic benefits without someone or some group bearing the costs. A tariff is a tax.

For professional groups, another approach is offered. It is usually in the form of *licensing*, which is a grant of monopoly rents to those inside the protected profession. The profession elects representatives who sit on government boards, or who actually make up the whole board. They can police entry into the profession's ranks by unqualified competitors, meaning those who have not passed certain educational and/or skill requirements established by the board. Most professionals believe that such restrictions on entry are entirely natural for the sake of preserving the present-day standards of practice that the majority of the profession accepts. Like the businessmen, they see these benefits as normal, natural, and altogether beneficial to the public. Result: higher fees and fewer choices.

Another way to buy off almost any industry or professional association is by means of *direct grants of money*. The government may simply buy products from a company. It may establish government research grants. It may subsidize certain industries directly. In the case of the great railroads in the United States which were built in the 1860s and 1870s, the government offered millions of acres of land to the railroad companies as an incentive to begin and complete construction.

Perhaps the most popular form of subsidy is *tax relief*. Certain occupations, companies, or organizations receive tax breaks. In an era of growing taxation, this approach has been one of the most effective; the higher the tax level, the more advantageous is tax exemption. The American oil industry was the recipient of multiple tax breaks until quite recently, and they are still substantial.

All of these special favors are adopted in the name of the general welfare of the public. All of them involve the financial incentives for private individuals and firms to conform themselves to the goals set forth by the sponsoring agency, the government. All of them involve the transfer of wealth from consumers and taxpayers to the beneficiaries. All of them involve a temporary suspension of market forces and a redirection of those competitive pressures. All of them necessarily involve a reduction of the sovereignty of the recipients, since they become partially dependent on the government for continued benefits.

In short, the bait is most tempting

Setting the Trap — Extra-Market Costs

The government is a political organization. Its justification is that it is an agency of the popular will, an agent of the public in its political capacity. It is therefore an agency of public defense. The general public is to be protected from adversaries, including domestic adversaries. In a limited-government system, this means that those who use fraud or violence against their neighbors are to be penalized. In modern interventionist states, the concept of public defense is much broader.

The government cannot lawfully make grants of power or money to any group unless it is in the public interest to do so. In short, the state must police those it subsidizes. The money cannot be used exclusively for the benefit of private citizens. The long arm of the law is at the end of the strings attached to every grant of monopoly power or special favoritism. In theory, every dollar spent by the government must be accounted for, to make sure that the public's interest is upheld in each expenditure. The result, among others, is an endless proliferation of forms.

The state grants a particular group special favors. But it cannot do so randomly. It must have a purpose, officially and unofficially.

The official purpose is not nearly so important as the unofficial purpose. The official purpose is offered to calm the public (which must finance the grants) and to make sure that the judiciary does not intervene. The unofficial purpose is almost universally this one: *the expansion of political power at the expense of private associations.*

Once the grant has been made, the beneficiaries use it for their purposes. The money is spent. Parkinson's Law takes over: expenditures rise to equal income. But expenditures are always difficult to reduce, especially in large, bureaucratic organizations. The firms become used to the higher income. The income becomes part of annual forecasts. Managers expect it to continue. After all, they are all agreed that such subsidies are in the national interest. Would the nation (the politicians) revoke their trust? Never! The organization is hooked. It has become dependent on the continued favors, meaning the continued favor, of the state.

Inevitably, one firm or some individual begins to take advantage of his position. He exercises the monopoly grant of power which the state provided for him. He charges a bit too much. He starts running a "factory." Or the firm or individual cuts quality. In short, someone actually begins to milk the system.

The Patterned Response

Some of us have become cynical over the years. We have so often seen this pattern, and the government's equally patterned response, that we have been inclined to come to a startling conclusion, namely, that *the government establishes the system in order that some beneficiary will milk it.* That is a primary purpose of the system of government favors.

Once the pattern of "exploitation" is detected by citizens or government officials, not to mention bureaucrats at any level of government, the response is politically inevitable. Someone calls for the government to do something about the unfair use which is being made of the government's trust. Some firm or some professional must be stopped, and stopped now.

The industry or guild must be policed. The consumer must receive protection from the unscrupulous. The industry leaders naturally resent this intrusion into the semi-free market. They resent the fact that someone is milking the system. That person, for one thing, is trying to get more than his "fair share" of the booty. Also, he is making the government angry. He is threatening the continuation of the subsidy. He is violating professional standards.

This appeal to professional standards is very important. The government knows what appeals to make, and this is a good one. (The industrialist is not nearly so alert to such violations, since the agreed upon standards are not so clear.) The ethics of the professional association are at stake. They must be defended. Yet it is extremely expensive to enforce standards on a colleague. Friendships are at stake. Careers are at stake. Yet a small percentage of incompetents (usually said to be about 3 per cent by every representative of the professional association) threaten the semi-autonomy of the group. (There is no real autonomy if the government has granted some sort of favor.)

Needs for Policing

The government demands that the industry or professional group police itself. The market as a policeman has been compromised by the original grant of power or money. This compromised policeman—the consumers—cannot enforce its decisions inexpensively, given the government grant. So the government calls on the group to police itself, and it draws up certain standards that should be met. The "partnership" between government and professionals grows strained. So the industry or professional group elects (or more likely accepts) certain spokesmen who will "work with" the other partner. This supposedly will insure that the interests of the government and the favored group will mesh, and that the group will continue to receive its favors. On this point, I can do no better than to quote Enoch Powell, a Member of Parliament in Great Britain. He makes quite clear what the industry can expect.

They start more than half-beaten, by the very fact that they are, or claim to be, the spokesmen and representatives. It has been their pride and occupation to "represent" industry to the Government. Yet the safest posture for an industry confronted by Socialism would be not to have an organization or spokesmen at all. Instead of being able to coax, browbeat or cajole a few "representative" gentlemen into co-operation, the Government would then, unaided and at arm's length, be obliged to frame and enforce laws to control, manage or expropriate a multitude of separate undertakings—the true picture of private enterprise—with no means of getting at them except the policemen.

Powell is here speaking of an industry which is not on the receiving end of major government favors. If government has the industry

on a string, it need not have to resort to the policeman. All it needs
to do is to cut off the subsidies, and the whole industry is put into a
financial crisis. The existence of the subsidies calls forth the "industry's spokesmen." And to quote Powell, "As soon as 'our President,
Lord So-and-So' is in a position to talk about what such-and-such an
industry 'wants' or 'thinks' that industry is on the road to the
scaffold. . . . The Association of these, the Federation of those,
present just that one neck to the Socialist garrotter."[2] Once the government uses the bureaucratic garrotte to strangle the representative
of the industry who stands in place of all the members, there is no
way out except to repudiate the compromiser who stuck their collective necks into the garrotte. If they do not pull out their own necks,
they will suffer the same fate.

The professional guild is perhaps the most vulnerable, since the
very nature of the "bait," namely, a monopoly position based on
guild-policed licensure, creates the very policing organization necessary for the government to impose its will at lowest cost. They can be
appealed to on the basis of professional standards and the guild's responsibility to a vaguely defined public, irrespective of the individual
professional's ability to satisfy the needs of specific members of the
public.

Springing the Trap—Extra-Market Crisis

More cheaters are discovered. The guild waffles. The cheaters
continue to operate. The press scents blood and headlines. Politicians scent blood and votes. When they look into the actual operation of the industry, they find more examples of men or firms that
have gouged the public, meaning people who are taking advantage
of the very system that the government created—an eminently ex-
ploitable system. So the reports of cheating and fraud continue. The
reports continue, but no prosecutions are begun by the government,
since nothing specifically illegal has been detected. The guild is
powerless, obviously, for the same reason. This means that the
reports are going to continue. The guild will still be under pressure

---

2. Enoch Powell, *Freedom and Reality* (London: Batsford, 1969), p. 46. It must be
understood that Powell is discussing the traditional response of so-called establishment guilds. He does not deny that breakaway splinters from these established
guilds might be able to create a minority resistance on the basis of ideology and
long-run self-interest.

to do something to stop the causes of the reports. Finally, new laws are called for to clean up the industry, since the industry is seemingly incapable of policing itself.

For professional associations, this is a disaster. Members have been led to believe that there are standards of practice within the profession. Yet, these reports keep hitting the front pages. Their self-esteem is challenged. They begin to wonder what has gone wrong. Maybe the reports are correct. Maybe the government needs to do something — not anything drastic, of course, but enough to clean up the temporary mess and let honest men continue to practice. They miss the point: *the government's task is to alter the practice of the honest men.* The government wants to set all standards and enforce them. There will then be no doubt about who the senior partner is. Bureaucrats want control.

The crisis is not created by the negative reaction of consumers. Businessmen do not find that one morning sales are down 30 per cent because the public has decided to walk away from the fraudulent segments of the industry. Professionals do not find their offices empty for weeks on end. In short, it is not the market which drives home the message to the supposedly crisis-bound industry or profession. The critics come from outside the market, probably from those who seldom use the products or services involved, or if they do, who find the products or services quite adequate in their particular cases. But the crisis is no less real, for the public and even members of the associations perceive it as a crisis. This means that the crisis is real politically. "Politically" is what counts in an era which is socialist or interventionist in its economic outlook.

What about the representatives of the industry? Will they co-operate? Powell answers straightforwardly:

You bet they will. They are afraid not to. They are afraid of being pilloried by the Government and its political supporters as "unpatriotic" or simply (damning word) "unco-operative." They feel that the eye of the public will be upon them, and they do not like the adjectives which they foresee would be liberally used inside and outside Parliament — and will be, anyhow, before the end of the day. Of course the line of true patriotism would be the opposite to the one they are going to take. It would be to protest, by all means in their power, short of breaking the law, against every kind of error and nonsense as it comes along, and to oppose in their own industry any measure which does not commend itself to their knowledge and experience. But they shrink from this because, although they have no seats to lose and no voters to offend, it takes courage of a special kind—political courage—to outface authority and the popular cry of the hour. These men have commercial courage, and no doubt physical courage too; but facing the political music is something they have neither been trained nor volunteered for. So they play along with the search for an incomes policy, or export incentives, or whatever else it may be.

And, as Powell points out, "The effect is doubly damaging; for it also hamstrings any politicians who *are* prepared to raise their voices in protest." The public thinks it strange that industry representatives have not protested the accusations by the government. Apparently, the leaders approve of the government's policies. "Thus the co-operators effectively expose the flank of the anti-Socialist opposition and compel it to fall back on positions which are better protected."[3]

But not much better protected, he might have added.

Once the crisis is admitted to exist by the leaders, though of course, on a much reduced scale—3 per cent of our members, not 20 per cent—the battle is pretty well lost. To clean up that 3 per cent, the government will alter the entire foundation of financing, policing, and pricing of the industry's service. The corruption will escalate, but now it will be a government problem, to be met by even more intervention. More laws can be passed, more penalties handed out, more regulations enforced: the government expands its control relentlessly. The trap has been sprung.

Skinning the Victims—Extra-Market Bankruptcy

There are any number of ways that the government can see to it that the former subsidies now become the strait jacket for the former beneficiaries. The most obvious method of control over professional groups is the establishment of government control boards that will enforce standards and privileges. The government begins to finance the guild more directly. The former monopoly grant now becomes direct payments. But these payments have no strings attached; they are ropes, or even chains. The government sets fees, allocates equipment, and assigns consumers (clients). The government directs the operation of the association through its captive agents, the profession's representatives. Members of the profession are told what they will be paid, the kind of service to be offered, and the quantity of service to be dispensed.

---

3. *Ibid.*, p. 47.

The government also establishes some sort of quality-control standards. These are enforced by quality-control boards made up of compliant members of the profession and representatives of the public (pressure groups) and the government (bureaucrats). These quality-control boards do exactly that: *control quality*. If quality, meaning cost, starts going up, then they step in and control it. They ration equipment. They set lower standards of care, especially in government hospitals or clinics. They make sure that costs are held down, since the government, not the consumer, is paying the bill. No matter what guild is involved, the government makes sure the "irresponsible quality" is avoided, meaning irresponsibly *high* quality.

The government forces industries to operate at a loss. The classic example in economic history is the American railroad system. Created by government subsidy, controlled in the name of protecting the consumer, the railroads in the Northeastern part of the U.S., as well as the Midwest, have been strangled to death. The Interstate Commerce Commission was the first Federal regulatory agency in the United States, established in 1887. It was established in the name of protecting the consumer, but as the New Left historian Gabriel Kolko has argued, along with free market economists like Milton Friedman, the result was a freezing out of new competition, since the ICC established rate floors as well as ceilings. So the railroad barons were already in trouble by the late 1880s, despite the millions of dollars in subsidies. The "protection" became a stranglehold, and by the late 1950s, the passenger-carrying railroads were in trouble. By the early 1970s, they were bankrupt. The government now owns and mismanages many of them (Amtrak, Conrail). (Long-haul freight railroads are still able to compete.)

The incomes of the members of the industries and professions that are now directly financed and/or directly policed by the government necessarily fall. Envy is loose in the land. The popular press and television reporters have accomplished their goal. The public will not permit "profiteering." The politicians will not permit it. Prices, wages, and fees are controlled, and work loads increase. Regulatory agencies each claim a piece of the action, and the multiplication of paperwork is endless. The formerly independent producers, who answered directly to the formerly independent consumers, now answer to a multitude of bureaucrats and enraged customers who detect the collapse of productivity on the part of the now-controlled suppliers. Most suppliers lose, most consumers lose, and a real crisis is produced.

Conclusion: Avoid the Bait, Rely on Principle

The answer, philosophically, is to avoid sniffing at the bait. This must be done on principle. It would help if businessmen understood the chain of events which follows from the acceptance of a government subsidy. Yet even if this chain of events is not understood, men should still be able to recognize a violation of basic moral principle when they see it. They should understand that the coercive power of the state should not be used to benefit one group at the expense of another. Such power is inevitably misused, if not immediately, then ten years or fifty years down the road. The precedent is evil; the results following it will also be evil.

The problem, as indicated by Hayek's statement which introduced this chapter, is that businessmen like the seeming safety of a government-restricted market, at least in the early stages, when they are given some power to set standards and direct production. Businessmen can make very good bureaucrats, too. The market is relentless. It forces men to meet the demands of a fickle public. Businessmen think they can find an escape in some sort of government-business partnership. That is the grand illusion.

Those who are offered the subsidy must say no very early. There are strings attached to government money or power, and they become chains if the subsidies are allowed to continue. It is easier to say no before the addiction process begins, before costs rise to meet income levels. The longer a violation of principle continues, the more difficult the "withdrawal" process becomes.

5

BIG BANK BAILOUT—
THE VULNERABLE FDIC

There are a lot of people who know how to sniff around and dig up significant information. I received a letter from a subscriber who had taken my advice when I wrote several years ago that I thought that locksmithing would be a good skill to pick up. He went to school, got himself certified, and now has a locksmithing business in the north-central U.S.

He received a mid-week phone call one evening. It was a supervisor of the Federal Deposit Insurance Corporation (FDIC). My subscriber was asked to come and switch the locks and keys at a local bank. The bank had just gone belly-up. It was a local bank in a small agricultural town.

The next day, he was called back to secure some business properties that the defunct bank owned. The FDIC had made an offer to a larger regional bank to allow it to buy the assets of the defunct bank. The other bank took the deal. My subscriber was curious. He had read Remnant Review long enough to learn how to sniff around. One of the best ways is to play dumb while playing sympathetic, the "Gosh all whillikers, you sure must be overworked, and by the way, how do you operate?" routine:

While I was working on these extra buildings the next day, I started asking questions as innocently as I could to the FDIC team supervisor. But I really only got one question out because the answer so stunned me, I couldn't think of anything else all day. I said to him, "It must be mass confusion to you guys when all of a sudden you have to rush out and get a bank back in shape like this."

He laughed and said, "It used to be that way when we had about 15 of these a year to do. But now we do about 15 a day, so the experience is vast." They apparently have something close to an army of crews to go out on a moment's notice if need be.

My question is: Can this possibly be true or is this guy exaggerating a bit?

My opinion is that the official was exaggerating. If you have 15 locked banks per working day, that's 300 per month, or 3,600 per year. If it were that bad, I think the story would get picked up by the Democratic Party, the Washington press corp, and various other news media. So I don't think it's that bad.

But the supervisor's major point ought to be accepted at face value. It used to be a novel event to go out and close down a failed bank. It isn't a novelty any longer. Regional banks, especially in agricultural communities, are shutting down at a rate unprecedented since the great depression.

At this point, the FDIC's bureaucrats have got to be running scared. Their reserves are increasingly tied up. No one wants to buy the assets and liabilities of Continental Illinois Bank. Who can blame them? If another major bank goes under, Congress or the Federal Reserve System will have to intervene and make the funds available. Short-term money is exceedingly short term today. It can happen overnight. We've seen it happen. This is not a needless scare story.

The bank insurance programs for banks, savings & loans, and credit unions operate in terms of the assumption that the U.S. Government or one of its licensed monopolies (the Federal Reserve) will step in and bail out the insuring agencies. The FDIC and the FSLIC have about 1.3 cents and one cent respectively in reserves for every dollar that is insured. The credit union reserves are even less. What keeps the system afloat is the faith people have in the government to bail out these unofficial agencies that are not legally tied to the revenues of the Federal government. Yes, Congress passed a joint resolution in 1981 which guaranteed bank deposits up to $100,000 per deposit, but a joint resolution is not law. To be law, it has to be signed by the President. No such law has ever been signed, although in a crisis, I think it would be passed into law. My point is: perception rules events, at least most of the time.

What the FDIC has done, in effect, is to short the money market. It has promised to deliver money that it doesn't have if there is a crisis. But if we get another Continental Illinois Bank type situation, the FDIC won't be able to cover its short position. It won't be able to deliver. Someone else has to come in and cover the short position.

The Lender of Last Resort

Everyone knows who this is. It's the Federal Reserve System. Everyone thinks the FED will cover the FDIC's position. Almost everyone believes that in a major crisis in the Eurodollar market, the FED will be forced to cover there, too, in order to protect the European branches of American banks. Furthermore, if the FED were to refuse, it might bring down the whole European banking system. It might lead to a new world depression.

So we have thought in the past. But I want to offer a few warnings in advance, while there is still time. I have begun to consider some alternative scenarios that I have yet to see discussed in print. Please bear with me.

I once had an interesting discussion with Richard Band of Personal Finance. We began to speculate (intellectually, I mean) about the ways that the FED could bail out the system in the case of a major default by Third World debtors. As I was flying home, I got to thinking about the whole problem. A lot of pieces started falling in place that had eluded me before.

Yes, the FED will take action. The question is: What kind of action? We're all trying to second-guess the FED, and it isn't easy. Before I begin this exercise, let's consider a few propositions. I think we have to accept these if we are to be able to make anything more than a wild series of guesses.

1. The FED was the 1913 creation of major New York banks.
2. The large multinational banks still dominate FED policy.
3. The FED will not knowingly act against these interests.
4. The large multinational banks rely on the FED's monopoly.
5. Multinational bankers have taken major risks on this assumption.

We have been told for a decade that the exposure of the lenders to a default by Third World nations is very great, and that the banks that rely heavily on earnings from foreign loans are too vulnerable. Yet they have continued to escalate foreign loans. Were the lenders stupid? Would they willingly take such risks in a competitive market? I don't think so. They have adopted the attitude of the insured lender: "I'll make as much as I can for as long as I can, and when I can't make it pay, I'll ask for a bail-out which I know I can get." That's what the central bank is for. That's what central banks have been for since the late seventeenth century. That, and their other major task: making loans to the governments that license their monopoly position.

Banks such as Citibank, Chase Manhattan, Manufacturers Hanover, and Bank of America derive anywhere from 50% to 75% of their total earnings from income from foreign loans. These are the TBTF banks: too big to fail, or more properly, too big to be allowed to fail. They have enjoyed a monopoly in these foreign lending operations because they know that the FED won't let them go under. Their potential American competitors don't have this assurance. They stay out of the foreign markets, leaving a fatter share for the multinationals.

But if a coalition or consortium or cartel of foreign debtors gets together and agrees to a unilateral default, what then? We are talking about Mexico ($110 billion), Brazil ($110 billion), Argentina ($75 billion), and any others that want to come along for the ride. Not all of this is owed to U.S. banks, but probably a fifth to a quarter is. We are talking about a quarter of a trillion in bad loans that could become visibly bad overnight. This is vastly more than the capital base of the European and American banks that have made the loans. Brazil suspended payment in March of 1987, threatening the West's banks. The cracks in the system are showing.

Those of us in the camp of the inflationists have believed that any attempt to bail out these banks would be either highly inflationary (the FED creates the monetary reserves or prints the money directly) or highly deficit oriented (the Congress borrows the money from the public to bail out the banks directly). We have assumed that the system as a whole would be supported. We forgot the major monetary insight of Ludwig von Mises: inflation (fiat money) enters the market at specific points. It distorts the market as it spreads throughout the economy. It is not a matter of everyone getting the new money simultaneously. It is a matter of certain people getting their hands on the money before anyone else can.

People watch the FED very carefully. People also understand where price inflation comes from. It comes from monetary inflation, which in turn comes from increases in reserves. When the FED buys a money asset, the monetary base increases. Reserves increase, and banks that sell the FED the asset in question can loan more money than before. Banks that get fresh deposits from beneficiaries of the FED-Treasury coalition can also make more loans. Monetary inflation strengthens the position of the banks that get earlier access to the new fiat money. Monetary inflation does not strengthen the position of the banking system as a whole; on the contrary, it weakens it.

It also makes some banks more vulnerable than others to changes in the business cycle when the FED finally tightens money (e.g., 1980-82, 1984).

If the FED pours in money, it will break the dollar internationally. It will also alert Americans to the next round of inflation, which millions of us expect. The FED is caught in a bind: it must disguise the nature of the bail-out.

Scenario Number 1: The Discount Window

The default is announced by the Third World debt consortium. The now-insolvent multinational banks line up for loans from the FED's discount window. What would they use as collateral? Their dead loan agreements? If so, see Scenario Number 4. If not, so much for this scenario — the one that the newspaper financial columnists would probably predict.

Scenario Number 2: The FDIC Intervenes

The FED intervenes through the FDIC. Will Congress object? Why? Either the FED bails out the big banks, or Congress does, and then takes the political heat. Congress's self-appointed chief task is the avoidance of political heat.

The FED creates new reserves by buying up FDIC assets. The FDIC issues paper promises to pay, and the FED buys them. This is now legal (Monetary Control Act of 1980). Or the game is played by way of the off-budget Federal Finance Bank. It makes no monetary difference. It would be inflationary. The FED would monetize reserves. This would pour billions of dollars of new assets into the banking system, by way of the New York banks. This is the standard prediction of the inflation-predicting newsletter writers. Or if they don't actually predict such a scenario, they implicitly assume it. I used to believe it. I don't any longer.

The FDIC enters the picture and takes over the big banks. But the FDIC can't possibly run these banks. They haven't got the skill. Only the FED itself would be big enough to buy up these assets and skilled enough to run the banks. This is why I think that this scenario is unlikely. It would be politically difficult to allow the existing bank owners to maintain control over the assets. The FED's bureaucrats would become the legal owners of the big banks.

This is why the kind of conventional FDIC bail-out that we read about in the newsletters is probably unworkable if there is an overnight default by Third World debtors. The "powers that be"—that really be—wouldn't accept the consequences. They will maintain control over their banks. Remember my initial assumption: that the FED exists for the sake of the American multinational banks, not the other way around.

Scenario Number 3: Printing Press Bailout

This would be the FED's response if a true bank run were to begin. It would mean printing up money by the hundreds of billions. It could happen, but it's a last-resort position, for it would clearly be inflationary and the end of the road for the banking system, meaning the world monetary system. They will go to great lengths to avoid this one, the scenario in Paul Erdman's *Crash of '79*.

Scenario Number 4: Swapping Reserve Assets

This is my guess. Say that a dozen major banks are facing bankruptcy because of an overnight default by the consortium of Third World debtors. A run on the banks threatens to ensue all over the U.S.—both an internal "Telex" run and an external "line up in front of your local bank" run. The FED wants to avoid both. It is afraid of printing up massive amounts of currency to send to banks all over the country. Everyone will know that the move is inflationary. The metals markets will boom, and everyone will renew his hard money newsletter subscriptions. The folks at the FED don't want that.

So the FED gets smart. The major multinational banks will be sitting on top of mountains of dead assets, namely, promises by Third World debtors to repay. But the promises are broken. The capital assets are gone. So the FED offers a very sweet deal: "We will exchange our T-bills for your Third World loan receipts." No new monetary reserves come into the system. No new money is created. The FED gets one paper asset in exchange for another.

What do the banks get? The most sought-after liquid asset on earth: the T-bill. These can be relied on to earn a high return, or they can be sold to the general public. There is a cost involved, however. While the FED repays about 85% of its earnings to the Treasury each year—$15 billion or more these days—commercial banks don't repay. They keep the money. The operational (though not the accounting) Federal debt therefore jumps by whatever the face value of the transferred T-bills is. Someone has to pay the extra annual interest expense. "Someone" means us.

There will be a hue and cry against this swap unless it is done during a national emergency. The public has been prepared (orchestrated) by the news media since 1981 to interpret a Third World repayment moratorium as a national emergency. But what will the FED do with a pile of promises to repay by Latin American bankrupts? Who cares? Not the FED. They sit on a pile of paper promises anyway. They return 85% of the booty each year anyway. If the government stands ready to keep the FED's doors open (nationalize it), what do the FED's bureaucrats care? If the major multinational banks are sitting on a pile of easily marketable, high-paying T-bills, what do they care? Sure, they may "lose ownership" of the FED. So what? They don't own the FED for the dividend payments the FED pays on the stock. They own it in order to be bailed out of a crisis and to manipulate the money markets. The former bailout will have been delivered on schedule. Why not "give up ownership"?

This swap would reliquify the multinational banks — the American multinational banks. Meanwhile, the European multinational banks will be lining up to their central banks to get the same deal. But they will not get dollar-denominated assets; they will get only domestic monetary assets, if they get anything at all. The FED has no obligation to act as their lender of last resort. Thus, the whole Third World debt scam has benefited certain exporters (who sold the debtors the goods) and the American multinational banks. It now threatens the European banks with third-rate status. In short, the transfer of banking power has almost taken place: from London, Frankfurt, and Zurich to New York and San Francisco. Conclusion? The big bank insiders want a controlled default! It's risky, but if they win, they win most everything.

But, you ask, "What kind of rip-off is this? The American multinational banks will get the FED's T-bills, and we taxpayers will foot the interest payment bill." True, but who will complain? Most of the populist critics of the FED think the FED keeps all the interest money anyway, so they won't spot the nature of the transfer. They will be no angrier at the system than they are now, and no more effective politically. The European bankers will scream, but what political clout do they have in the U.S.? Their screams will be a political asset to the American multinationals. The FED will be sitting on dead assets, and some congressmen may complain, but remember: this will be done in the middle of a national emergency. Congress will vote for it. After all, they voted for the Monetary Control

Act of 1980, which authorizes the FED to hold non-T-bill assets. The fear of a banking collapse is too great.

The FED can then be safely nationalized. At the point of nationalization, its assets will be worthless. Its bureaucrats will be kept on the payroll. Its good assets will already have been transferred to the American multinational banks. By nationalizing the FED, Congress will placate the FED-haters. And then we will know why it was that Times Books (owned by the New York Times) was willing to publish Maxwell Newton's excellent critique of the FED, called simply, *The Fed* (1983).

Meanwhile, until the consortium defaults, the American multinational banks can sit tight, drawing their quarterly interest payments from Third World near-insolvents. So: heads (no default), American multinational bankers win, European multinational bankers win, and foreign debtors lose; tails (default), American multinational bankers win, foreign debtors win, European multinational bankers lose, and American taxpayers lose. But the key fact is: American multinational bankers win. Take your pick.

Scenario Number 5: Publicly Admitted Insolvency

The default comes. The New York banks are declared insolvent. The government does nothing. "Take your lumps, dummies; you made the loans." The banks default on all deposits, including all the local banks around America who put money with the multinationals. The money supply contracts by about 80%, and the entire world economy goes into a deflationary depression. The New York bankers admit their error, and they all enroll in the University of Nevada, Las Vegas, to study economics with Murray Rothbard. And, best of all, subscribers out of gratitude all renew Remnant Review by paying in tenth-ounce Krugerrands. Then I buy Chase Manhattan Bank and become an insider.

Conclusion

The banks will continue to get taxpayers to finance, "nickel and dime," the repayments by insolvent Third World debtors through the IMF, the World Bank, or direct foreign aid. The FED may even resort once or twice to buying up newly issued Third World debt in order to allow the debtors to maintain interest payments to the multinational banks. But this helps the European multinationals, too. The best scenario from the point of view of the American multinational banks is a co-ordinated default by the foreign debtors, a declared national emergency, followed by an asset swap with the FED. If they can get away with it politically, they will achieve their goal: the ultimate bailout. The American multinationals will be made fully liquid (T-bills), the taxpayers will foot the bill (interest), the bankrupt FED will be nationalized (pleasing the FED-haters), and the European banks will be turned into third-rate institutions. The United States will become the banking capital of the world. The transfer of banking power will be complete, worldwide and domestic.

6

CLICHÉS AGAINST GOLD

Today, people are talking about gold. Back in 1967, nobody talked about it except people like Harry Schultz, Bill Baxter, and a handful of skeptics. Then came Harry Browne's book, *How You Can Profit from the Coming Devaluation* (1969), followed two years later by the devaluation. Sure enough, those following Browne's advice—advice criticized widely by the professional economists, investment counsellors, and government experts—made a pile of money. Nevertheless, the same old clichés are still heard today. The same tired explanations of why gold is such a poor investment are put into print by the same tired critics, who are still telling their readers and other victims about the "loser's game" of gold and silver. Here are my favorite anti-gold explanations.

Gold is too speculative. Let us quote the former dean of the anti-gold bugs, Eliot Janeway. Janeway is a genius, and there is no doubt that anyone who has read his columns for ten years, and did precisely the opposite of what he has recommended, is a rich man today. Janeway's track record is fantastic: the only jockey in the pack who races his horse clockwise around the track. It's faster, he says. Back in mid-December of 1976, when gold was in the $130s, up from its low of $103, someone wrote in and asked what he thought about buying gold. Janeway was the man who predicted in the late 1960s that once gold was severed from the dollar, it would fall from $35 per ounce to $6. He was *the* expert in gold. So he replied: "When you have an asset—like gold—which pays neither interest nor a dividend, you are not investing; you are speculating." The fact that *all* forecasting, *all* investing in terms of a forecast, is speculating, is ignored by Janeway and the other "gold is speculative" experts. When you invest in something that pays you a return you are speculating that the outfit you just loaned your money to won't go bankrupt, that it will continue the dividends, etc. Whenever you are in the stock market (or "in" anything else), you are a speculator.

It should also be pointed out that in times of monetary and political turmoil, he who refuses to take speculative risks is condemning himself to a loss of capital, though perhaps on a slow, paralyzing basis rather than the big loss all at once. If the rate of price inflation is 13%, your 7% 2001 bond or your 9% first trust deed is eroding your capital daily. He who "invests" (meaning he who remains in conventional, acceptable, "prudent" speculations) is lost.

But Janeway was not content to rattle the old "speculation" bones. He never is. He always has to get specific, which is where you can make a bundle by going the opposite way. Therefore, said Eliot: "As far as gold goes, it is a bad time to buy. The late 1976 gold play was a flash in the pan. Gold won't enjoy that kind of move again as long as Russia and South Africa are plagued by their current economic troubles, and dumping their surplus." Well, gold is up, there is still trouble in the USSR, and South Africa is under the worst external pressure in half a century. That's Janeway. His advice appeared in the *Washington Star* (12/16/76).

Gold is just another commodity. This has been very big in recent years. The economists have specialized in this one. It has been considered one of the richest of the anti-gold veins. Now that gold has been severed from the dollar, it has not stayed at the old $35/oz. price. It has gone up and down (as priced in dollars), just like any commodity. Gold is metal, just like copper. So why get so excited about gold? Why make gold into a religion?

Well, they are correct as far as they go. Gold *does* go up and down. Gold *is* a metal. Gold is indeed a commodity. And in times of high price inflation and currency disintegration, the other metals will be just like gold: skyrocketing in price. So why all the fuss about gold?

Here is one very good reason: you can take a British gold sovereign almost anywhere on earth and buy valuable items with it. People make a fuss about gold precisely because people have *always* made a fuss about gold. Moses, in the second chapter of Genesis (2:11), made a fuss about gold. It *is* a commodity. It is *the* commodity. It serves as money because it is portable, durable (nothing destroys it except aqua regia, an acid), divisible (in its pure form, a knife can cut it), and scarce in relation to its weight (high marginal utility per ounce). It is also very lovely to look at. Gold is the Sophia Loren of commodities. I can almost hear former Secretary of the Treasury

William Simon now, looking at Miss Loren and then pointing to a picture of Zazu Pitts and exclaiming, "After all, Sophia Loren's only a woman, like any other woman." All right, Bill, since we're double dating, *you* escort Miss Pitts.

Let's try some other variations. "After all, the Rolls Royce is just another car." "We ought to remember that David Rockefeller is just another banker." "Face it, the Council on Foreign Relations is just another discussion group." "Really, Notre Dame is just another football team." "Kareem Abdul-Jabbar is just another center." "Chairman Mao was just another agrarian reformer." I'm sure you can come up with several of your own. Send them to Bill Simon, Just Another Ex-Monetary Expert, Washington, D.C.

The key element of money is its *continuity over time*. A person will voluntarily exchange scarce economic resources for money only because he expects others to do the same in the future. The fact that a particular monetary unit or form has served as money in the past helps to convince him that it will serve as money in the future. This is one reason why I don't think that the government will revalue the dollar by forcing us to exchange 10 or 20 of our old dollars for one new dollar, a "redback" for 10 or 20 "greenbacks." The reason why people are not suspicious about our declining currency is because they are used to it. They don't know anything else. It has served as money for too long. So old habits are not easily broken. It is only if the old habits are finally broken by monetary chaos, when prices have climbed to astronomical levels, that the government is likely to revalue the currency by knocking off two or three zeroes. As I have said before, it could happen in a national emergency, when the government rations our money back to us, in order to make worthless cash that might be hoarded by the suspicious types (like me) in advance of the Federal freeze on bank accounts and safety deposit boxes. That's why I recommend keeping one or two month's cash reserves outside the bank, but other reserves in silver coins and gold coins. If the government should revalue the currency, it would probably not be any advantage to be holding greenbacks — not in comparison with gold and silver coins, anyway.

Gold offers continuity in exchange, worldwide. Silver coins do in this country. So buy a "bag" ($1,000 face value) of pre-1965 dimes and put your other "speculative" coin money into gold coins. *Get yourself some monetary continuity*, precious metals, that cannot be easily counterfeited by Federal inflationists. If your friends want to trust in the continuity of paper money, let them. I prefer to believe in another, far more ancient and historically reliable continuity, namely, the continuity of fiat money inflations whenever governments depart from precious metal coinage.

Buying gold is unpatriotic. This argument was used on the Greeks just prior to World War II. The Greek government called on its patriotic citizens to turn in their gold coins, accept the government's paper money, and live happily ever after. Greeks, having had considerable experience with democratic governments, hoarded gold anyway. Those few who did act "patriotically" saw everything lost when the Nazis invaded and subsequently stole the gold while debasing the Greek currency. According to one friend of mine, whose uncle was involved in the operation, the U.S. used to fly missions over Greece, dumping high quality counterfeit money over the side of the planes, thereby compounding the monetary crisis. Those who hoarded gold survived far more easily. Moral: "But if any provide not for his own, and specially for those of his own house, he hath denied the faith, and is worse than an infidel" (1 Timothy 5:8). Your allegiance is to your family before it is to the bureaucrats and professional confiscators who infest the seats of government.

What *is* unpatriotic is allowing the government to exercise the monopoly of money creation. What *is* unpatriotic is to encourage the debasement of money by permitting the creation of money unbacked (unrestrained) by precious metals. What *is* unpatriotic is to allow the planners to use the control of money as the tool of directing the economy, whether by Keynesian fiscal manipulations (always inflationary) or Friedmanian monetary "stability" (always inflationary). Whether the money supply is pushed up at a Keynesian rate of 8% or Friedman's 5%, the money supply is still compounded, and if you compound any figure at any positive rate over time, it becomes exponential, soaring into the heavens, or, in the case of the purchasing power of money, diving into the gutter. Government planners can no more resist the lure of comprehensive planning through monetary manipulation (debasement) than university economists can resist the lure of unrealistic assumptions.

What *is* patriotic is the preservation of capital. What *is* patriotic is the willingness of men to plan for their own futures, not relying on the confiscatory power of governments to guarantee the futures of all major voting blocs. What *is* patriotic is thrift, intelligent speculation (forecasting), and the setting aside of resources that will facilitate both personal prosperity and the restoration of voluntary trade should price controls and rationing destroy the division of labor and per capita wealth in this country. If a person saves some coins for the future, in the rational expectation that someone else will want to trade resources for some coins, he has not hurt the country; he has only made the coercive plans of the bureaucrats more difficult. *What's good for the country is bad for the bureaucrats.*

You can't eat gold. When you hear this one, you know you're dealing with a person who can't distinguish horse manure from apple butter. There is a good answer for this one: "You can't eat Federal Reserve Notes either." Other things you can't eat: New York City bonds, Penn Central shares, Equity Funding insurance returns, Argentinian annuities, and CD's in the Bankhaus Herstadt in Germany. You can't even eat 1975 WIN [Whip Inflation Now] buttons. But you can buy food with gold.

The government may outlaw gold. The government may also outlaw freedom. This is the reason a person buys gold. It is because bureaucrats and politicians think they have the moral and legal right to interfere with the voluntary decisions of the citizens of any nation that the citizens are wise to invest part of their assets in commodities like gold and silver coins. The government also outlawed gold coins in 1933. Interestingly enough, we can still buy $20 gold pieces (double eagles) in any coin shop. Why? We are fairly certain that the coins in Fort Knox were melted, since some of the gold there (the gold that the Congressional investigating team was shown back in 1975) was admitted to be coin melt. This means that the coins that we can buy in the open market are coins that were *not* turned in back in 1933. It means that the President called for gold in 1933, but gold didn't come when it was called. Not all of it, anyway. Probably not most of it. That was in an era when people trusted Presidents. That was in a period when people believed in the Federal government. Can you imagine the response of those people who have bought gold since 1965? Gold today is bought, not as present money, but as *future money*; not as a present medium of exchange, but as a hedge against government policies. The psychology of gold holding today is completely different.

What if the government should outlaw gold? It could be done by means of the emergency powers held by the President. But to implement these powers, he will also have to implement a whole ocean of Federal regulations — regulations that will require an army of bureaucrats. The very implementation of a comprehensive planning program will make it almost impossible (and very expensive) to implement any single component of that program. They will go after guns, I think, before they go after gold. Then, after their ranks are thinned out a bit, they may decide that those holding gold are also those who hold guns, and frankly, it's easier to write up reports for a living, with the accent on living. In any case, governments have always resorted to banning gold when they have tried to implement total control, and men have always disobeyed.

Anyone who believes that the government might try to ban the ownership of gold has just offered the best argument for buying gold: you can't trust governments.

However, I doubt that the government will make the attempt. First, they have spent a decade to convince us that "gold is just another commodity." If so, then why abolish it? Why alert people to the fact that it is *the* commodity? More important today is the fact that in late October 1977, President Carter signed legislation which included the reintroduction of the right of Americans to make contracts in gold. This had been illegal since 1934. In other words, the final trace of the New Deal's restraints on gold has been abolished. To abolish gold, apart from an executive order, the Congress will have to reverse itself. Congress usually takes a generation to reverse itself, as the gold clause contract legislation indicates. Usually, it refuses to reverse itself; the men are too busy devising new cures to people's problems. So I conclude that Sen. Helms' gold clause legislation put nails into the bureaucrats' attempts to restrict gold ownership. Emergency powers could pry out these nails, but without very serious economic conditions, I don't think Congress will bother. I don't expect Americans to use this new freedom to make gold clause contracts, at least not for many years, but the freedom is significant nonetheless. It is symbolic of the end of the New Deal gold laws. Freedom is now the political precedent.

There is one aspect of this threat, namely, that government may abolish the ownership of gold, that is significant, at least theoretically. The government may (I believe will) freeze the legal price of gold in the cash (spot) markets and in the futures markets. In other words, I think *all* commodities will be put under the price freeze, including futures prices, at some point. I think it could come in the early 1990s. I could be wrong. Naturally, it will destroy the whole market system of production and distribution. Of course, it will create havoc. Certainly, it is an *insane idea.* That's why I think it's coming.

Ultimately, I think the inflation tax, secured by the legal tender laws, will be coupled with a price freeze. If it is comprehensive, it will have to involve the futures market. The Nixon Administration did not freeze futures last time, and that "mistake" will not be made next time, or at least not through the whole period. If futures prices are left free, there will be a rush from the conventional capital markets into commodities — thereby creating havoc in the government's attempt to keep prices low. Admittedly, I am painting the worst scenario possible. But I am convinced that the slogan of all price controllers in the future will be this: "No more Mr. Nice Guy."

I would still not be a long-term creditor, not with a gold clause, silver clause, or any other kind of clause. The clause must be tied to U.S. paper money, and U.S. paper money is controlled by U.S. paper politicians. Legal tender is monetary tinder. No long-term credit position can be protected while these words are on our money: "This note is legal tender for all debts, public and private." The long-term debtors will drown the long-term creditors in fiat money, and the number-one long-term debtor is the Federal government.

What I'm saying is this: *legal technicalities like contracts will not hold the juggernaut State.* By all means, use contracts to buy a little protection. Better a gold clause contract than no gold clause contract. Use every device that you can to defend your freedom and your capital. But don't be naive: we are living in an era of *legislated envy.* We are living in an era of judicial lawlessness. We are living in an era which favors the criminal at the expense of the victim. When envy is the ethics of the day, paper contracts will not defend your long-run capital from paper money. Keep your credit position short. A three-year loan to somebody else is extremely long run, justified *only* because of tax considerations (e.g., taking a contract on a piece of property you're selling). Even then, I think it's questionable. Pay your taxes, convert the paper money to hard assets, and forget about "passive" income. *Passive income is actively threatened by fiat money.*

If the government outlaws gold, you'll become an outlaw. It's as simple as that. If they outlaw gold, it will be because of their desire to put the whole nation into jail. They will force everybody into the black markets. Selling anything at a price close to a market price will also be illegal. If all voluntary transactions are declared illegal, you might as well keep your gold coins. If you're going to be an outlaw, be a well-heeled one. Gold will then steadily become a black-market money, but as far as I'm concerned, the reason why we buy gold coins is to gain access to a black-market money. Buy now, spend later.

Gold can go down. True. Response: gold can also go up. (You would be amazed at how stupid some of these clichés really are, yet they are written up by the experts.) The propagandists want us to believe that "gold is just another commodity," except that unlike other commodities, gold doesn't go up as often as it goes down. In other words, "gold is just another commodity, except it's a poor investment."

The government may dump more of its gold. Let's hope so. Gold is getting too expensive for me. I want some bargains. When the Treasury runs out of gold, then the price will go upward once again. There will be one difference. I will have my gold, and the bureaucrats in the Treasury won't, at least not in their official capacity. I'm into gold for the long-haul. If anyone wants to sell me gold at a discount, I'm the long-term beneficiary. Why let the government get the capital gains from a gold price rise? Let them sell it at bargain prices to U.S. citizens, and let them reap the capital gains. Isn't that what we want, gold in *our* hands and not in government's hands? Let them dump to their heart's content. I'll buy some more. Let's face it, where gold is concerned, I can do no better than to cite the immortal lines Burt Lancaster uttered in "Vera Cruz." The "heroine" offers Burt and Gary Cooper a deal: $3 million worth of gold, split 3 ways. "That's a million dollars' worth apiece. That's enough for anyone." To which Burt replies: "Not for me; I'm a pig."

The government may go back to a gold standard. This is supposed to be an argument against holding gold for the long haul. If the government really did go back to a full gold coin standard, with 100% redeemability of dollars for gold, *and refused to abandon the policy,* then gold would indeed prove to be a poor investment. But the reason we hold gold is that we do not believe that the government will return to a full gold coin standard. We do not believe the government would stick to it even if it did go back. At best, there could be a *temporary* phony gold standard, supported mainly by mirrors and smoke. If so, this would be an ideal opportunity to add to your supply of gold, while the public loses interest in gold.

Losing interest in gold. Gold does not pay interest. Thus, conclude Keynesians, Friedmanites, and other conventional economists, people should not hold gold. The problem with this argument is that it ignores what happens to money during mass inflation.

In the fall of 1985, when the Mexican peso was at 250 to the dollar, Congressman Dick Armey's aide (at my suggestion) called several economists with the Federal Reserve System, and asked if they thought that individual Mexicans were holding cash dollars as an alternative currency—an inflation hedge. They assured him that this was highly unlikely, since Mexicans could not earn interest on cash dollars. Three weeks later, the peso was at 500 per dollar. Those professional economists—idiots all—had ignored the obvious: Mexico's mass inflation. A year and a half later, the peso was at 1,000 to the dollar. Any Mexican who held dollars instead of depositing the money and getting paid interest on his pesos had preserved 75% of his monetary wealth compared to those who deposited the money. Today, of course, most economists who study the Mexican economy admit that cash dollars do serve as an alternative currency, even though dollars do not pay interest.

Conclusion: economists who do not live under mass inflation are lousy advisors when the economy becomes inflationary.

The economy today is not inflationary. From 1980-1986, the U.S. was in a disinflationary mode. Precious metals were not good investments throughout most of this period. But the cost of this disinflation was the worst recession since 1940 (1981-82), huge tax increases, and the worst peacetime budget deficits in U.S. history. The willingness of Americans to buy Treasury debt is what allowed the system to escape from monetary inflation. But the debt is becoming too large to service without rising interest rates. To keep rates down, the Federal Reserve System will have to continue to inflate the dollar. Unless the government takes the Federal budget into surplus, using the extra money to reduce the Federal debt, or else repudiates this debt openly and also refuses to provide fiat money to bail out the banking industry, there will be mass inflation. As I write this, the House Banking Committee has just voted to recommend that Congress appropriate $5 billion to bail out just the Federal Savings & Loan Insurance Corporation. Thus, Congress will not default on the U.S. directly. Congress will default indirectly: by inflating the dollar.

The economy will again become inflationary. The dollar will collapse.

Gold will not save you if the dollar collapses. This is correct. If the dollar collapses, we are talking about social chaos. On the other hand, neither will paper money save you. Gold will make the chaos somewhat more bearable. Paper money and T-bills and bank accounts will provide almost no protection. Gold will allow you to buy survival goods in emergencies, but more to the point, if you buy survival goods today and store them, you may not have to touch your gold in the worst of the crisis. After the crisis has passed, gold will still be money. Dollars will not be. Gold can help get you from now to then, and also leaves you with something of value in reserve when "then" arrives.

Conclusion

Can the Federal debt increase year after year by $150 billion or more? Of course not. Does Congress show any signs of cutting spending? Of course not. Does Congress ever act responsibly when it comes to spending? Of course not.

Conclusion: "go long" gold and thereby "short" Congress.

7

VALUABLES DURING HYPERINFLATION

Investment strategies are very complicated affairs. A conventional investor is always concerned about capital gains (as denominated in his national currency) and income (also denominated in paper currency). The price he is willing to pay for an asset is, assuming the investor is rational, the present market value of the expected future income stream, discounted by the expected rate of interest.

The unconventional investor ought to be looking at capital gains and income flow, but he has another dimension to consider: alternative currencies. In a time of increasing government intervention, we can expect a flight of capital out of the strictly currency-denominated investments into the "alternative money"-denominated investments.

It is incredibly difficult for conventional investors to rethink their attitudes toward money. Everything they are familiar with in the conventional markets is related to the domestic monetary unit. Yet it is risky to lock one's future income stream into currency-related investments. The currency units of the world are not to be trusted. They are government monopolies, and shrewd men do not trust government monopolies.

Even unconventional investors find themselves slipping back into the thought patterns of conventional investors. I am constantly amazed in my discussions with hard asset-oriented people at the extent to which they have remained infected with the "traditional wisdom" of conventional investing.

Let me offer an example. I talk with people who have invested substantial proportions of their assets into gold coins. They will then measure the extent of their financial wisdom by the appreciation of the dollar price of gold. Yet these same people would not be willing to sell their gold at today's price. They expect further appreciation. Fine, but why use the dollar as the measuring device? Isn't the dollar

exactly what gold buyers are trying to escape? Isn't the total unrelia-
bility of the dollar the heart of their investment philosophy? Yet they
persist in thinking of the value of gold in terms of its dollar-
denominated price.

Shouldn't we consider, instead, the collapse of the dollar in terms
of its gold-denominated price? Shouldn't we be thinking in terms of
one four-hundredth of an ounce of gold, compared with the former
value of one thirty-fifth of an ounce?

It is far easier—meaning far more conventional—to measure
gold's value by the quotation in dollars. But this consideration
should be acknowledged in advance by the unconventional investor
as a kind of shorthand. Naturally, it is valid to quote so many dollars
per ounce, but a person who is trying to flee from dollars should
never make basic investment decisions in terms of gold and dollars
as such. He must rethink his philosophy. He should be thinking in
terms of gold and dollars and something else.

"Something Else"

I am not trying to be cute. I am trying to crystallize your
thoughts. I am trying to get you to think through the implications of
your own philosophy of investing. It really does matter what you
think about your assets. You have to decide just what it is you're trying to accomplish with your capital.

Gold and dollars and something else: here is the necessary formula for capital preservation. The dollar is money, meaning an acceptable medium of exchange. "Medium" means intermediary. You
sell goods for dollars. You are not after dollars; you are after goods
and services. Dollars are simply a shorthand for economic calculation, a shorthand without which all modern economies would collapse, since the division of labor requires an acceptable medium of
exchange. Fiat currencies provide these accounting standards in the
world today. You may prefer to measure your capital gains in terms
of dollars, but the more inflationary the economy becomes, the more
erroneous your shorthand calculations will become. You should
always keep some idea of the purchasing power of the dollar in the
back of your mind when you start calculating your capital gains.

If you consider your profits in gold, they should be hard asset-
denominated profits, adjusted by the capital gains tax losses that you
may be paying. If you convert from gold to dollars to assets, you will
lose part of your profits when you pay the tax. If you pay the tax,

and intend to continue paying it, then you should always discount your profits mentally, so as to not paralyze yourself when it comes time to sell out. The conversion from gold to dollars to something else involves a loss. If you tithe, it involves a further reduction in assets. Never forget this.

All right, what are the implications of the "gold to dollars to something else" formula? Most important, you have to answer this question: "What do I intend to do with those future dollars?"

You would be astounded to learn that the majority of gold coin investors have never really thought this through. They are stuck in the mental straightjacket of conventional investment categories. And by "they," I mean you.

When do you intend to sell your gold? When the dollar-denominated price reaches what level? If you have never considered this question, you are in trouble. To answer it, you should consider the following factors:

1. How fast does gold hit this dollar-denominated price? (Will it push even higher?)
2. What are the prospects for war at that time?
3. What is my income for that year? (tax considerations)
4. What can I do with the money at that time?
5. What is the future of the dollar at that time?
6. Is it still legal to buy and sell gold without leaving records?
7. Are the same economic policies that created price inflation still in effect?
8. Has gold become an alternative currency unit on markets that I deal with? (black markets)

People invest in gold for conventional reasons, of course. They buy gold futures contracts, never intending to take delivery of the actual physical gold bars. They put gold away for a few years instead of opening a bank account. They use gold as collateral in some sort of loan transaction. But I am not talking about the semi-conventional uses of gold. I am talking about unconventional investing.

What do you intend to do with the gold coins? Sell them for dollars? Barter with them? Those are the only choices (other than selling them for some foreign currency). You are after future goods and services, agreed? But how do you intend to buy them? With gold or paper money? This is the heart of the "gold to dollars to something else" equation. Will it really be an equation? Will the entries on all sides stay fairly constant? Will gold = paper money = goods during the time frame of the conversion process?

If you are acting rationally, you will not sell your gold for money unless you trust the stability of the dollar's purchasing power during the conversion period. The sale of gold means that your faith in the dollar, at least temporarily, has been restored. You want "something else." Are you more likely to be able to buy it by holding gold or paper money? Which is money for you? Which is your medium of exchange? In short, what are you predicting about other people's assessment concerning gold and dollars in the future, namely, at the point when you convert to "something else"?

Remember, you're not after money, a medium of exchange. You're after the things that the medium of exchange will purchase when you decide to buy.

The best way to keep from getting hypnotized by gold, buffaloed by gold, dizzied by gold, and ultimately dumped by gold, is to keep in mind that gold is a potential medium of exchange. As conditions change, the usefulness of gold as a medium of exchange will vary. You are after "something else." You must time your actions to enable you to get the greatest quantity of "something else" with your gold or paper dollars

Some Myths of the German Inflation

There are endless stories about how much gold would buy during the worst months of the great hyperinflation in Germany in 1922-23. More and more, I am beginning to doubt them. Unless I can get primary source documentation, I have a tendency to dismiss them as myths. Why? Because other data, both theoretical and historical, point in the opposite direction.

We believe that our modern productivity stems from the division of labor in a free market. Yet we also know that the destruction of reliable money inhibits the division of labor. Bad money drives out good markets (North's revision of Gresham's law).

When money is no longer reliable, people have great difficulty making accurate assessments of the value of capital or any other economic resource. When information costs rise, the economy is crippled more and more. Yet it is money, within the framework of an unhampered price system, which is the most stupendous conveyor of information ever developed by man. Profits and losses are measured in terms of money. Destroy the relative stability of money, and you destroy economic calculation. (For an interesting and useful discussion of the accounting implications of this fact, see the book, *Economic Calculation Under Inflation*, published by the Liberty Press, 7440 N. Shadeland, Indianapolis, IN 46250: $8.95.)

Why, then, should we believe that in general, the person with gold coins was able to buy important goods — important in the conditions of 1923 — with gold? If the destruction of the market was the inevitable result of mass inflation, why should we think that mere pieces of yellow metal were sufficient to overcome all the terrible losses of efficiency associated with the breakdown of a modern market economy? Is gold magic? Are gold bugs the new magicians? Or is the heart of our prosperity the existence of unhampered markets and personal freedom?

Let me refer to a most remarkable book, *When Money Dies*, by Adam Fergusson. It was published in London in 1975 by the little-known firm of William Kimber & Co. It sold for five and a quarter pounds. It is a non-technical study of the great inflations of Germany, Austria, and Hungary in 1923. You can probably still order a used copy from Blackwell's, Broad Street, Oxford, England, a firm I have dealt with successfully for many years. Fergusson cites a letter from Sir Joseph Addison, the Chargé d'Affaires in Berlin for Britain, dated September 11, 1923:

> Unknown heights have now been reached. The floating debt increased this morning by 160,000 milliard (billion) marks. Efforts to calculate in something else are vain; it all comes back to paper marks. The shops are demanding pounds, francs, Danish crowns and any other foreign currency you may care to enumerate, and then take half an hour ascertaining how many thousand millions they require in paper marks: hence an increase of prices quite beyond the fall in the mark. Except for things like tram fares, we are now charged for most articles a few hundred millions more than the same would cost at present exchange rates in London. It is natural, for the shopkeeper discounts a further fall. He has become unaccustomed to thinking in simple figures, so it is thought that forty or sixty shillings must be nothing without millions at the end of them. The Adlon Hotel charges the equivalent of 4 pounds or 5 pounds for a bottle of wine. . . (pp. 176-77).

Fergusson adds in a footnote concerning the price of wine in Berlin: "Ten or twelve times the London price: a bottle of good claret at the Savoy Hotel in 1923 cost about 10 shillings." Ten shillings made half a pound sterling.

What this means is that for the average purchase, the average man would have been far better off living in London with his pile of gold coins or stable foreign currencies. It was the freedom of the market and the stability of money in London that made daily living less expensive, even in terms of gold, than in Berlin.

I am reminded of the story related by Prof. Donald Kemmerer concerning his father's interviews of Germans for his famous studies of the German inflation. (His father was Prof. Edwin Kemmerer of Princeton.) He asked the same question of many Germans: "What could you have done to make things better for yourself in spite of the inflation than things would have been had there been no inflation?" The answer was always the same: "Nothing." Sure, food storage would have helped, or some dollars, or some gold, but ultimately, almost everyone lost.

Naturally, some sharp bargainers were able to make those spectacular trades that we read about, though perhaps they were not that spectacular. There are always successful entrepreneurs who have the right asset to trade when another person is desperate. I am talking here about average people in their daily exchanges. It was here that men lost more by the disintegration of money than they made by their ownership of gold or dollars (which was the universal measuring device for the mark—the dollar-mark exchange rate was announced daily and then hourly).

The people who did better than most were the peasants. They had food to sell, and they were favored by the below-market interest rate loans of paper marks that were made possible by the huge outpouring of marks by the German central bank. (On the final day of the inflation in November 1923, the call loan rate for money on the stock exchange was 10,950% per annum, while the central bank was still charging 905.)

What was observed in all three of the defeated nations should stand as a warning to all of us: the steady transfer of formerly valuable assets to the peasants. And once the crisis ended, those formerly valuable assets become valuable again. Consider the diary entry of January 1, 1919 by Ann Eisenmenger, a widow of a former middle class husband in Vienna. If we expect the worst of the various scenarios, we should look at these words, not the nonsensical hopes of the more utopian goldbug newsletters, as the most likely results of mass inflation:

Even the most respectable of Austrian citizens now breaks the law, unless he is prepared to starve for the sake of obeying it . . . The fact that the future is so uncertain has led to stagnation in industry and public works, and swelling numbers of unemployed supported by the State . . . yet it is impossible to get domestic servants or indeed any sort of workers. . . .

Heightened class-consciousness is daily being instilled into the manual workers by the Socialist government, and, in heads bewildered by catchwords, leads to an enormously exaggerated estimate of value of manual labour. Only in this way could it come about that the wages of manual workers are now far higher than the salaries of intellectual workers. Even our otherwise honest old house-porter is demanding such extravagant sums for performing little jobs that I prefer to do the heavier and more unpleasant household work myself. . . .

I survey my remaining 1,000-kroner notes mistrustfully, lying by the side of the pack of unredeemed food cards in the writing table drawer. Will they not perhaps share the fate of the food cards if the State fails to keep the promise made on the inscripturation of every note? The State still accepts its own money for the scanty provisions it offers us. The private tradesman already refuses to sell his precious ware for money and demands something of real value in exchange. The wife of a doctor whom I know recently exchanged her beautiful piano for a sack of wheat flour. I, too, have exchanged my husband's gold watch for four sacks of potatoes, which will at all events carry us through the winter . . . When the farmer's eyes rested on the grand piano at which Erni [her blinded son] was seated improvising, he took me aside and said: "My wife has been wanting one of those things for a long time. If you'll give it to me, you shall have all you want for three months". . .

There was a steady stream of pianos, furniture, family heirlooms, gold watches, jewelry, and gold coins toward the farms and a stream of food flowing the other way. We are talking about the breakdown of the national division of labor. We are talking about the disintegration of money and the markets that money made possible. It was food, not gold, that was king.

What does the term "valuables" mean? Gold, silver, jewelry, precious stones? Why do we call them "precious"? In short, what are "valuables"? It depends upon external circumstances and the evaluations of buyers and sellers concerning these circumstances. Forget about "intrinsic value"; start thinking about market value. Consider the words of Judith Listowel, a Hungarian:

My relations and friends were too stupid. They didn't understand what inflation meant. They didn't rush to get rid of their money (that was what the Jews and the Germans did). All my relations thought it would stop the next week—and they went on thinking so.

They woke up very late. They started selling their valuables because they couldn't buy food—the china from the mantelpiece, the furniture, the silver. That made them think—it made them think when the price of a set of old silver spoons went up from 20,000 to 40,000 crowns in a matter of a week or two. And if you had to sell a valuable writing desk for money which was worth only half as much as a week later, of course there was ill-feeling.

It was resented when Jews bought these things. The Jewish women would turn up at parties or at the dansants when we were all broke, wearing silver fox furs—three at a time for ostentation—and diamonds which they had bought from our relations for a song—or what, when they saw them again, had become a song. My relations didn't know the value of anything. They were stupid. Our solicitors were no better. My mother's bank manager gave her appalling advice—he didn't know what he was talking about either.

She was not an anti-semite. Indeed, she was a liberal who was shocked at the rising anti-semitism that was produced by the inflation. But one stupid display seems to lead to another, and then back again. This ought to be a warning to anyone who has assets in a time of crisis. Keep them hidden, and don't be arrogant.

The Jews had been badly treated in Hungary since the 1860s, and were not received socially for many years. Nine out of ten bore grudges, and when the opportunity of impressing the arrogant gentiles arrived at last, who was to blame them for taking it? When they made a success of inflation, they were hated. When they were ostentatious about it, they were hated even more. It may have been stupid of them, and of course the wiser Jews, especially the older ones, were greatly upset, and remonstrated with the younger, because they foresaw the antagonism their behavior would create. . . .

Ultimately, there were no winners. Hitler proved that well enough.

One Possible Strategy

With this as the background, I come to the main point. What do you intend to do with your "media" of exchange? What will you do with your gold coins? Will you barter on a narrow, inefficient, possibly illegal market? Or will you sell gold for paper money? Will you hold through the inflation, the controls, and then sell in a deflation or recovery period? Or will you try to sell out at the top, meaning the bottom of the dollar's slide? You had better decide soon.

To illustrate a most important use of fiat money—the repayment of debt which is denominated in paper money—I return to Fergusson's narrative.

Herr Hans-George von der Osten, who had formerly flown with Baron von Richthoven's Flying Circus and was later for a short time Goering's ADC until he shot the Reichmarschall's favorite stag, recollects that in February 1922, with a loan from a friendly banker, he bought an estate neighboring his own property in Pomerania for 4 million marks (then equivalent to about 4,500 pounds). He paid the debt in autumn with the sale of less than half the crop of one of his potato fields. In June of the same year, when prices were shooting up ahead of the mark, he bought 100 tons of maize from a dealer for 8 million marks (then about 5,000 pounds). A week later, before it was even delivered he sold the whole load back to the same dealer for double the amount, making 8 million marks without raising a finger. "With this sum," he said, "I furnished the mansion house of my new estate with antique furniture, bought three guns, six suits, and three of the most expensive pairs of shoes in Berlin—and then spent eight days on the town."

This was simple commerce: the only thing to do with cash by that time was to turn it into something else as quickly as possible. To save was folly. Von der Osten was a piker. Had he waited one year, he could have paid off the debt on his estate with the proceeds from the sale of one potato or one egg. He could never have bought the shoes, antiques, and other goodies with the paper money generated from the sale of one potato, however.

What would have been the best strategy? He should have bought the antiques, guns, shoes, and so forth by borrowing even more on his farm from a private lender or a commercial bank, and then paid off the debt a year later with that single potato. Meanwhile, he could have bartered his potato crop for even more furniture.

Conclusion

When a society creates an economic environment where such profits and losses as these are possible, it has pursued immoral monetary policies. We have to face squarely the realities of confiscation through mass inflation. We have to understand how the system operates and how to defend ourselves against it. People who look at money income, instead of "goods and services income," are generally destroyed by inflation. This, unfortunately, involves millions of people.

Prices rise because people bid up prices by means of fiat money. Everybody falls behind — almost everybody — because of the disruptions in exchange and production produced by the insecurity and instability of money and contracts. The fact that it was cheaper to live on gold in London than in Berlin in 1923 testifies to the devastating effects on productivity that monetary inflation can produce. Real income falls for almost everyone because real production falls. Mass inflation produces inefficiencies that reduce the purchasing power of money even more than the mere increase of monetary units. Thus, at the end of mass inflation, prices rise even faster than the percentage increase of money. Not only is demand (as measured in money) increasing, but supplies are decreasing (lower productivity). Prices skyrocket. Increasing quantities of money raise prices, and decreasing supplies of goods and services also raise prices. The economy gets "the double whammy."

What I want you to understand is this: pieces of yellow metal are helpful in mass inflation, but they are not cure-alls. We need durable goods during such times. We need them, first, to guarantee ourselves a steady stream of goods, since we remove ourselves from full dependency on the market supply system. Second, we need goods in order to keep us from having to sell our gold, silver, and heirlooms in order to eat and survive. On the far side of disaster, we will still have our metal capital and our heirlooms. We don't have to dump our silver and gold coins at a discount in relation to food, simply because we will not be buying food during the crisis.

Your gold, in short, should not be aimed at getting rich in mass inflation. It should be used as a survival reserve, as a form of capital that will be valuable on the far side of disaster, and as a means of gaining access to paper money that can then be used to pay off debt and pay taxes. But gold is not to be thought of as a means of buying up valuable items — valuable during a crisis, anyway. It may be used for buying up items that won't be valuable during a crisis (pianos, old paintings, antiques, etc.), but which may appreciate after the crisis is over. But for such purposes, food and basic necessities will be much more useful than gold.

8

DEBT: PLAYING WITH FIRE

Long-term debt is one of the disasters of the twentieth century. The availability of easy credit, such as 20-year, 30-year, and now even 40-year mortgages, all guaranteed by taxpayers through the FDIC, FSLIC, and the Federal Reserve System's printing presses, has converted the thinking of men to the logic of permanent debt. For some reason, men almost think of themselves as long-term debtors, which makes them easily susceptible to the lure of "a little inflation" per annum, in order to relieve them of their debt burden. They vote in terms of the psychology of debt, that is, how to skin those so foolish as to have become long-term creditors denominated in fiat dollars. Yet the grim reality is that most of the productive people of any society have become long-term creditors, though for some reason they never understand the implications of this fact. They own rights to future payments in dollars (Federal Reserve Notes): annuities, cash-value life insurance policies, bonds, mortgages, pensions, and various social security programs.

When I say that people do not understand their position as long-term creditors, I mean that they do not recognize these investments as long-term credit investments. If they did, they would not be so ready to commit their capital to such sure-fire losers. I have pointed out the danger of such investments for years, as have other hard-money newsletter writers, yet when I speak with people concerning their present assets, they are proud to point out to me how much they have "saved," they think. They have, in fact, given away capital assets to the inflation monster. Show me the person who says "I can't buy gold; I need income," and I'll show you a person who has not understood the nature of loaning present dollars in exchange for future depreciated dollars.

We have seen the transformation of earlier American investment practices, which were based on short-term credit (except for cor-

72

porate bonds), into the psychology of long-term theft. We have shown people the marvels of repaying with future depreciated dollars their present debt obligations. We have made the theft process of mass inflation acceptable, step by step, as we have redefined "a little inflation" as 2%, then 4%, then 6% per annum—always knowing that the present rate of price inflation is higher than the "acceptable" rate. We have shown two generations of Americans that debt pays— at the expense of ignorant long-term creditors.

The Bible affirms that the debtor is servant to the lender (Proverbs 22:7), and that it is best to be totally debt-free (Romans 13:8). Debt is for emergencies, and it should be limited to six years, maximum (Deuteronomy 15:1-6). The economy of the Bible assumes that there should be no inflation of the currency—honest weights and measures—and that long-term debts tempt whole populations to violate the prohibition against debased coinage (Isaiah 1:22). In such a non-inflationary economy, the borrower is indeed servant to the lender. Long-term debt, however, offers the debtors a way to escape, a way to make the creditors the captives: monetary inflation. The purchaser of an irrevocable annuity, for example, is easily captured, not the captor. (And, I might add, irrevocable annuities are the favorite traps issued by churches, seminaries, and other usury-peddling religious hustlers to the gullible members, all in the name of Christian stewardship.)

This being the case, I do not recommend long-term credit positions. But since I do not recommend that people offer others long-term credit, I do not recommend that people accept long term credit, thereby becoming long-term debtors. My rule is clear, stay out of debt, except in an emergency, and then accept no debt that cannot be paid off within seven years. Every man should strive to live totally debt-free one year in seven, minimum. This lets us keep the lure of "theft through inflation" at arm's length, and preferably farther. It also places on us acknowledged limits on what we can successfully forecast about future economic conditions. As the Psalmist said, "The wicked borroweth and payeth not again" (Psalm 37:21a). We should not shrug off massive personal indebtedness, which puts us at great risk of defaulting on the loan. Do not accept debt burdens that you do not think you can reasonably pay off within seven years. And take this debt burden only because you are convinced that we face an impending emergency.

This is not your run-of-the-mill investment advice from those who accept the grim reality of long-term inflation. But those who advocate massive personal indebtedness are really saying one of three things. First, we can perfectly predict the future, and we know that deflation cannot come, and that we will not, in our own individual positions, be whipsawed by the loss of job or income in a temporary recession. Second, even if we are uncertain about the future possibility of deflation, we can always declare bankruptcy and start over. Third, we might as well gamble on inevitable inflation, despite the precedent that successful "skinning of the creditors" sets for future generations. Since I accept none of these premises, I cannot in good conscience recommend long-term debt, even in a time of inflation. It may well be profitable in the short run. It may make it possible for a few people to make fortunes on other people's money. But it is not the way I think you build up an alternative culture to the disintegrating secular culture in which we find ourselves trapped. If we cannot offer decent alternatives now, what will we say if and when leadership is offered to us after the economy fragments? Our goal is long-term social reconstruction, not quickie profits through endless debt pyramiding. We are also trying to avoid personal bankruptcy.

Emergency Debt

We need capital. We need it to provide leisure in the future, a prerequisite for taking leadership. We need it to provide protection for our families. We need it to finance voluntary charities. We need it to increase our ability to master our environment through the division of labor. Thus, in a time of rapid, escalating price inflation and social disruptions, we need to increase the size of our capital holdings.

What do I mean by "capital"? First and foremost, I mean intellectual and moral capital. I believe in this form of capital because it is highly mobile—and because it cannot easily be taxed. Borrowing to provide an education is eminently sensible, if the training provided is really likely to be useful to the recipient. (Borrowing to get a Ph.D. in sociology is not so smart, in other words.)

Then there is one's home. This is the item that most of us have indebted ourselves long-term to buy. If a home is in a safe town, or if you are buying it for appreciation to enable you to buy a small-town house or small farm, then it seems legitimate. Rent controls will reduce our mobility. Price controls will make home construction risky, as construction materials will become scarce under controls.

The thought of being without a home in the future disruptions is unpleasant. A home is a legitimate investment, when it is suited to present and expected future needs of one's calling. High debt for social status should be avoided, especially when the envious start dropping by with torches.

Tools of all kinds are legitimate to buy on credit if there is no other way. These should be selected with an eye to the future. What kinds of tasks will be necessary in a period of reduced output, shrinking markets, social turmoil, and a reduced division of labor? These are the tools to buy now.

Gold and silver coins are legitimate capital investments. They should probably be purchased outright, however. These are to be held close to you in case of a panic. They are mobile. They are your long-term survival hedges.

We could go through several pages like this, but you get the point. It is best to pay cash. If you absolutely have to own something, pay cash (and probably leave few records). If you think you will need something, but you could survive without it, consider borrowing to buy it. If you don't want something repossessed, pay cash. If you don't want something confiscated, leave few records. For example, I would buy handguns with cash payments. I would not buy them with a credit card. But if I had to, I might buy handguns by taking out a signature loan at a bank, or a second mortgage.

One reason for borrowing on 90-day credit now is the establishment of a credit record that enables you to borrow more later on. Buy on credit now, even if you do not like debt, because in an emergency you will want to borrow to the hilt. I will give one important example. If price controls are imposed, you will have a few weeks to buy items on the shelves. You may only have a few weeks. You will have to make emergency purchases of goods that may have to last you for several years. Credit may be imperative under such circumstances. So you borrow now, always keeping money in reserve, and repay on time. Get your borrowing limit built up in advance. If you have an American Express "green" card, apply for a "gold" card: it allows you instant credit of $2,000.

To discipline yourself, always be sure that you borrow only for production assets like tools, or consumer goods that are durable and possible candidates for shortages in the near future. Be sure you have money in reserve, or liquid assets in reserve, or 99% sure income within three months, to pay off the debt. You are only establishing an emergency credit reserve — an established credit rating — not financing a buying jag.

Just remember December 8, 1941, the day after Pearl Harbor. On that day, the smart man started buying tires, spare parts, silk stockings for his wife (on the black market), a new car, tools, household appliances, and whatever else he could beg or borrow. It was then or never. On that day, it paid to have unused credit reserves.

Escaping Fiat Money

Don't swallow paper. That's my chief investing motto. Liberals much prefer "you can't eat gold," but mine makes more sense. Don't become the final recipient of fiat money. In other words, don't become a long-term creditor.

Let me offer a familiar example. Someone sells a piece of real estate. The only way he could sell it was to accept a note, such as a first mortgage, a second mortgage, or whatever. What should he do? He has three sane choices. First, discount the note for cash. Others may be stupid enough to want to become long-term creditors. Second, trade the note for more real estate. Third, go out and buy another piece of property on debt terms similar to those involved in the original sale. If you don't want to take the first two approaches, then don't sell the property for more than a seven-year note, assuming you have decided not to become a long-term (over seven years) creditor. But whatever you do, don't swallow paper. Better to serve as a funnel for paper money: you get paid by your debtor, and you immediately pass on the depreciating fiat money to your creditor. You wind up with appreciating real estate, not the depreciating paper money.

This leads us back to another of my formulas for economic survival: gold and dollars and "something else." You are ultimately after "something else." It's true, you can't eat gold. You also can't eat paper dollars. You're after something else. The question is this: Which is the most efficient, least expensive way to enable you to get ownership of something else?

When gold goes to $800 or higher, are you thrilled? If you're in the commodities markets, this needs no answer, since you're after dollars anyway, in the short run. But if you're holding gold for long-term appreciation, you should be horrified. Gold at $800 means we're that much closer to gold at $1500, and gold at $1500 means international currency panic, trade wars, possibly international war, price controls, shortages, and all the other "solutions" to long-term monetary inflations. When I saw gold shoot from $600 to $800 in a few weeks, I got a sick feeling. Is time running out? Gold is not like General Motors stock. You should not be ecstatic when gold goes up, since this means that the dollar—and with it, the world's reserve currency-based trading system—is going down.

I'm speaking here of gold held as a survival asset. I can think of one set of circumstances in which a rise in gold's dollar-denominated price might thrill me. If I were heavily indebted on a small farm, on which I intended to ride out any domestic crisis, and I found myself able to sell off a few gold coins, buy paper money, and pay off my debt on the farm, then the rise of gold's price would not be a direct threat to me. In such circumstances, I have allowed the panic in the gold markets to pay off my farm—to buy it outright.

In other words, I have escaped dollars. But I have escaped dollars more efficiently than merely by purchasing gold coins and holding them for appreciation, since "appreciation" is usually defined as dollar denominated price appreciation. But if other hard goods— food, tools, housing, etc.—are also rising in price rapidly, then the gold is less useful to me in my ultimate goal, namely, escaping paper money. This is the meaning of leverage. I wind up with more appreciating assets—gold, land, tools, etc.—than I would otherwise have been able to accumulate in a fixed period of time. Why? Because I have accepted the burden of paper-money denominated debt. Instead of relying on my annual income to finance my purchases, which means a frantic pursuit of rapidly appreciating items, I can rely on my forecasting skills to finance these purchases. In short, I have become an entrepreneur—a speculator or forecaster. Why not use these talents? Why rely exclusively on my wage-earning abilities to finance the emergency items that I need, or think I will need?

One answer why not is this one: I may guess wrong. I may forecast gold's rise in price, and deflation may hit, and I will find myself in debt without adequate reserves to pay it off. This is quite possible. It should warn us against massive personal indebtedness. Debt is a burden. But so is mass inflation with price controls. Here is our awful problem: How to escape the greater burden?

I recommend using compensated leverage techniques to enable us to accumulate survival capital more rapidly. Here is the basic approach. You buy an asset that is important to you, but not absolutely imperative. This may be a home, a farm, a set of tools, land, income-producing real estate, a business, or education. You finance it with borrowed money. Then you buy another asset which you expect to appreciate before your six years have ended. This is purchased outright. If the mass inflation hits, you sell off a portion of your back-up assets, "buy" money, and pay off the debt. For example, you decide to buy a farm worth at today's prices $100,000. You should then borrow as much of the purchase price as possible — say, 80%. You then buy a back-up asset, such as $30,000 in gold coins. Your goal is to sell off the coins in the midst of, or close to the end of, a period of heavy price inflation, retaining perhaps half of your coins in the deal, while buying the farm outright. You will have to calculate just how high the gold would have to go to enable you to accomplish this. You will have to decide whether you want a smaller farm or more gold, if you don't think gold will rise high enough to make this transaction possible.

If your area of expertise is real estate, and if the thought of national rent controls doesn't bother you, then you might use your real estate pyramid instead of gold. But if you ride the pyramid higher and higher, you should set a date for liquidation of a portion of the empire in order to gain access to fiat money that will pay off the existing debt. What you want is a debt-free empire, reduced through timely, principled sales of a portion of that empire, just prior to a deflationary currency reform, or at the end of your six years of debt, whichever comes first.

You are not trying to achieve the impossible with borrowed money. Every debt pyramid eventually topples. You must not adopt the philosophy of former multi-millionaire James Ling, whose empire toppled in the credit crunch of 1969-70: "This process can go on forever. Go in a company, buy it like we did Okonite, recoup your cash, and start redeploying again, constantly, over and over. There's no end to this." That's what the man said (*Newsweek*, Jan. 23, 1967). He also said: "I once heard a man brag about not having any long-term debt. That isn't a realistic attitude. On balance, it's always better to go to the money market" (*Fortune*, Jan., 1967). Results, as measured by L-T-V stock performance:

> 1962: $15 per share (1962 purchasing power)
> 1968: $169 per share
> 1970: $10 per share (1970 purchasing power)
> 1986: Bankrupt

Conclusion

Take some debt, if that's the only way you know how to get control of needed survival assets now. Take the debt with a stock of appreciating liquid assets to back up at least one-third of the total debt. Hope for an appreciation, in dollars, sufficient to enable you to: 1) pay off the debt; 2) pay capital gains taxes on the profits earned by the asset; 3) have some fraction of your original holdings of the asset still in your possession. I would use rare coins, income-producing real estate, antiques, art objects, collectors items, and other rapidly appreciating investments to serve as the compensation for my leverage. I would prefer to sell off these more speculative assets to gain access to the debt-liquidating paper money, rather than survival assets like Krugerrands, silver coins, or other directly barterable hard assets. You can live without antiques, art objects, and rare coins; you may find it too risky to sell off your "survival assets." Decide which portion of your assets should be used for compensated leverage, and which will be sold only in a total emergency (like that last .357 magnum round). You can keep records for those items that you eventually intend to sell for paper money. I buy speculative "penny gold" shares for this purpose. Paper shares to paper money is debt liquidation. I hope it works. Remember: this is an anti-inflation strategy. It should not be expected to work in time of recession, stable money, or deflation.

9

TURKEY SHOOTS

"It's as plain as the nose on your face." It doesn't take Cyrano de Bergerac to figure out that polite people should avoid these words. Nobody likes to hear that something important is right under his nose. The trouble is, that's just exactly where important things are likely to turn up.

It's a question of perspective. Or maybe it's timing. Then again, it's really a matter of experience. On the other hand, it's knowing the right questions to ask. Or a combination of the above. But the fact remains, when people get too close to a subject, they have an amazing ability to ignore the obvious. And the obvious resents being ignored. It strikes back in the most annoying and loss-producing ways.

Take for example a recent theory of stock market investing. The *Wall Street Journal* has written several articles about an investor who does extremely well, year after year, adhering to a very simple investment assumption: You can't make money investing in losers. His whole strategy is to develop predictive techniques that enable him to spot future losers. Obviously—there it is again—if everyone went looking for losers to avoid, the system would break down, since the market would discount the new information so rapidly that he couldn't reap his entrepreneurial profit. His forecasts would be less successful. Still, everyone is looking for those big winners, leaving the field of identifying the losers pretty much empty. It reminds me of that old story about the professor who attended the college beauty contest and spotted a young man who was intensely rating the girls. "Trying to pick a winner, young man?" he asked. "No, sir. I'm trying to spot a loser, so I can tell her how gorgeous she is. That gives me an inside track when it comes time to cheer her up after the contest." Everyone knows that you can't win with losers. So why is it that everyone leaves the field open to someone who simply makes money by eliminating the losers from his portfolio? It's as easy to profit from knowledge about losers as it is to profit from winners. But if you started an investment newsletter called, say, *Spot the Losers*, you would have trouble getting it started.

When people start dumping a stock or commodity, it's called profit-taking. Why not loss-avoiding? Somehow, people in the investment markets are lured by the glitter of profits, gains, increases to boggle the mind of Uncle Harry at the next family reunion.

There is an exception to this rule, however. If an item really isn't worth much, but someone gets it even cheaper, he brags. I can remember the response of a lady on a Caribbean cruise. I had just bought a rather attractive sea shell for $3. A lady came up and asked me how much I had paid. I told her. "That's a shame," she said, "I bought mine from one of those boys at the pier, and I only paid a dollar." She was quite proud of herself. And I, having been overcharged, was despondent. Of course the trip down there had cost her about $1,500 or so, while I had come with Howard Ruff's lecture team, and it had cost me an hour lecture. In any case, the sea shells were cheap compared to the cost of the cruise. But it was that percentage — 200% — that made the difference. We can all understand a bargain like that. (The capper came when another lady — who was loaded down with trinkets — commented on how my shell was chipped, which I would never have noticed, not being a skilled shell man. The real winners were the kids unloading the junk on us, and the owners of the cruise line, but everyone was comparing notes with each other to find out who got the real "bargains." The natives are returning the favor that was shown to them by our European ancestors to their ancestors several centuries ago: unloading trinkets on the dummies. The lady who had commented on my chipped shell later won first prize in the ship's masquerade contest by hanging all the trinkets around her neck and shoulders and writing "sucker" across her forehead. Everyone recognized the sagacity of her observation.)

We have to recognize our weaknesses. If we are less alert to loss-avoidance than profit potential, then we have to overcompensate to protect ourselves. We have to look at those avenues of loss avoidance more carefully, since that's where the average guy, and even the sophisticated investor, neglects his homework. (Now that I think about it, maybe it's only the sophisticated investor who is prone to neglect loss-avoidance. Maybe the average guy knows better.)

Where Will You Sell It?

There are a lot of pitchmen out there who are ready and willing to unload an overpriced turkey on you for a fat commission. Let me pass along to you North's law of investment turkeys:

The fatness of the turkey is in direct proportion to the fatness of the commission.

Clever, right? If I'm lucky, Allen Otten will quote it in a forthcoming *Wall Street Journal* column. The trouble is, it's true. The reason why the commission has to be fat is because the item does not have a ready resale market. That means that the investor is buying the sizzle, not the steak. The salesman is fattening up the pigeon with lots of talk about the huge profit potential in this "once-in-a-lifetime deal." He talks about all the potential, diverting the pigeon's eyes from the grim reality.

The buyer should be very wary of fancy brochures, especially color brochures. He should be wary about free dinners, and free trips to Desert Paradise, Arizona. The odds are, Desert Paradise, AZ, was more recently known as Prairie Dog, AZ, and soon will be known as Dry Heaves, AZ. You wouldn't believe that sixty years after the swamp sales boom of Florida collapsed in a wave of scandals, that the same swamp could be sold to unsuspecting buyers in New York, but it can be (and is). Why don't people figure out that free dinners touting real estate in Florida, New Mexico, and Arizona are a threat to their solvency? (I suspect that it's very hard to sell the same sort of land that is located in Nevada. Nevada is synonymous with gambling, and gambling is what the free dinner is all about.)

I used to do telephone counselling for Howard Ruff. I kept getting calls from people who wanted to know what to do about the land they bought in Florida, Arizona, New Mexico, or the Bahamas. I usually had to tell them to regard the money as a sort of unaccredited educational program's tuition fee. The school of hard knocks had just graduated another searcher after wisdom.

How can you protect yourself? Here's a rule of thumb so incredibly simple that it has sat there unnoticed, right under that proboscis of yours, for years. This tip could be worth tens of thousands to you. Oddly enough, it's something that won't make me famous in the newsletter industry, and I won't be able to use it in signing up new subscribers. Why not? Because it's a defensive investment tip-you know, loss avoidance. And loss-avoidance doesn't have much sizzle. But it can serve you as a shield in the future, and I can guarantee you that you'll never forget it. Here goes:

Find out how much it will cost you to sell it.

That's it. No muss, some fuss, and real protection. If you can come even close to answering this question before you sign the dotted noose, you will have a very good idea of what the item is really worth to you.

Let me give you a specific example. Say that you're looking at a piece of recreation property, i.e., dirt, rocks, and a few trees. This young man in the suede shoes is telling you that you have to buy today, that the price is going up soon, that this is, so to speak, the last train out. You should take the following defensive procedure before you sign anything. First, get to a phone book. Second, turn to the yellow pages under "Real Estate." Third, call at least three local realty offices and hit them with the following story. You're thinking about selling some land in the new Ecstasy Acres development. At this point, there will be a wild burst of laughter, some coughing, and the words, "I'll bet you are!" Fourth, you ask him what price per acre you could expect to get for the property you are considering. What you want to know is the amount of the discount—the price spread between what the suede shoe boy is asking and what the general public is paying. That's how much it will cost you to sell it. Get at least two opinions.

It is my opinion that in any real estate deal involving undeveloped land, if the price spread is greater than 20%, it's not worth your time. In other words, if you have to take a discount of 20% or more when you turn around to sell, you are buying sizzle. You have to take the discount because, simply, you're not much of a salesman. You don't have the money to invest in full-color brochures and free steak dinners. You don't have gleaming white teeth. You don't even have a pair of suede shoes. And when the potential buyer sees you, he'll start looking more closely at the land. Good-bye instant profit.

The reason why you should avoid most high-commission purchases is that you need liquidity in times like these. That means you want to be able to sell fast without having to offer a discount, or spend too much on advertising, or improving the property, and without having to offer some salesman a fat commission. You need to buy something, in other words, that has a wide, developed, open market, with a public exchange like the stock market or commodities market. You need lots of buyers and sellers, unless you are the man with special knowledge of the product, the local market, or future conditions. In other words, if you aren't the fellow with the suede shoes, stay away from the "golden opportunity."

Another example of this kind of investment turkey is the "instant collector's item, limited edition." It's limited mainly by the cost of running full-color ads. They have run out of presidents, great moments in sports, and state flowers on genuine china doorknobs. We're now down to the wives of vice-presidents and replicas of key United Nations votes on issues of concern to the Third World — all faithfully reproduced on silk flags, suitable for framing. But this set is "one of a kind." You only need to agree to buy one per month until sometime after the Second Coming in order to complete your set (and the terms of the contract).

Where will you sell it?

A simple question, really. Who is out there who will want a complete set (let alone a partial set) of Dwight D. Eisenhower watercolor facsimiles engraved on two dozen miniature brass spittoons? You must say these words to yourself:

"How can I be sure that a bigger fool than I will show up, cash in hand, to take this one-of-a-kind investment off my hands?" This is not to say that a bigger fool approach to investing never works. It does. You can buy shares of stock in companies that specialize in the production of items aimed directly at the biggest fools imaginable. They frequently use the subtle appeal, "You'll make a mint!" You may, but only if you buy their stock, not their reproductions. (And if they run out of fools, or fools run out of money — you know about fools and their money — then maybe you won't make a mint with the stock.)

But It's An Investment

Then why are you walking on it?

This is another variation of the "great reason to buy" pitch. The salesman, having spotted his mark, tells you that not only is this one of the last ones available, but it's also usable right now. You know, like a Persian rug. Or a new Mercedes. Something you really want because it fulfills a lifetime dream, or your sense of beauty, or your determination to impress Uncle Harry. But it's overpriced, and you know it. Worse, Uncle Harry will know it. "Another toy, eh, Billy? You never could resist a toy. Why, I remember that rocking horse you wanted, the one that lasted two weeks. . . ." So you take along the salesman's pitch, "but it's a great investment." The function of the pitch, basically, is to give you something extra to take along with you — an excuse for stupidity, poor planning, inefficient shopping, or just plain basic lust. It soothes the conscience. It justifies nonsense. "An investment, of course." And since you never intend to sell it, you'll never really have to test the validity of the theory. You'll never have to test your "investment" in the market.

If it's an investment, then at what price do you intend to sell it? What is your investment strategy? If you don't intend to sell it, then how can you be sure it's really an investment?

All right, a true antique may really be an investment. It may be a capital asset in time of an emergency. It may be a desireable item to pass along to the favored child. But it's an investment in the strict sense only if you are familiar with the secondary market for the item. It's your knowledge of the secondary market for the item, not the item as such, that makes it an investment.

I'm sure Harrah's auto collection is worth tens of millions of dollars. His antique cars are really one-of-a-kind. They are individually irreplaceable in some cases. But before he died, I noticed something significant: he didn't drive them to work. He didn't take week-end jaunts to Elko in them. They were investments. He treated them as such.

I used to get calls from physicians who wanted to buy a twin-engine plane. I was invariably told that it's just an investment. And, by the way, it's deductible. "Would you buy it if you didn't like to fly, and you could still make money with it by hiring a part-time pilot?" I asked. "Well, when you put it that way, no," was the usual reply. It really isn't an investment. It's a toy. It's a tax-deductible toy. That's fine, but why contact me for advice? I give investment advice. (By the way, if you're ever asked to take a flight in a private plane by a physician-pilot, regard it as the equivalent of an offer to take a drive with an ordained minister. Doctors think they are too smart to crash, and ministers think they are too holy. Few ministers believe in pre-destination, but they often drive as though they did.)

But I Need the Income

This is one of my favorites. This is the one that kept Milton Friedman and Eliot Janeway from buying gold — no income. If it doesn't pay a dividend, it isn't an investment. It's speculation. So they say.

Let's talk about income. First of all, as far as passive income is concerned, there isn't any. Not in an economy experiencing 10% price inflation. You may get 11% on your money, but you're taxed off the top, and what's left over doesn't keep pace with price inflation. In short, there is no passive income; there are only various stages of capital consumption. It's only a question of how fast you want to consume your capital.

If I buy an item, sell it a year later, and make 100% on my money, have I received income? As far as I can tell, I have. It wasn't passive. I had to make a decision to sell. I had to part company with the item. But I did certainly come out ahead.

What people want today, especially retired people, is passive income. They want to make a one-time decision and then sit back and enjoy life, income assured, decisions deferred, capital preserved. This is retirement thinking. It's suicidal.

Yes, many of them know that passive income is a myth. They also know they can't afford to retire. But they turn their backs and their capital on what they know, choosing instead a short-term fantasy world. They want to retire. They want passive income. They want it, and they're going to have it, and nothing I can tell them, including facts they already know, will dissuade them.

Why do retired people need income? You think I'm nuts to ask. Not at all. What I try to point out is this: they don't need *money* income. They need the items that dollars presently buy. They will continue to need such items. Then why tie one's hopes to money? Why not buy what you need in advance?

A person may have $50,000 investment capital. Why not take $25,000 of it and buy those durable goods that he or she expects to consume over the next five or ten years, and store them? Why not buy all the bulbs, kitchen utensils, consumer durables, paper products, frozen beef, frozen food, dehydrated food, new clothes or fabrics, sewing machines, thread and so forth? Buy and store. If a person needs more space, then he can rent a mini-warehouse. Pay a year in advance (ask for a 10% discount, of course). Mini-warehouse space isn't that expensive. There is the theft problem, but inflation is a more certain form of theft.

If the rising prices of everything exceed the return on conventional investments, then why don't people just sell their conventional investments and buy goods.

Isn't this obvious? Then why don't more people start buying this way? Why don't senior citizens form co-ops and buy goods in bulk at sharp discounts? Why don't they abandon their CDs, utility stocks, 8% municipals, and all the rest? Why don't they buy what they want, in bulk, in advance, on sale? Why don't they buy their future income by buying future consumption items? Why do they trust in the purchasing power of a monetary unit that is wholly untrustworthy? What is patently obvious has escaped them.

Sure, it's a hassle to shop now in bulk. It involves foresight. It involves active investing. Too many Americans are used to the idea of a guaranteed future, where everything they want will be available for money, including money that will be in demand. People have been lured into passive thinking. Their investing reflects their thinking. If a person is going to speculate — that is, deal with the uncertain future — it's a safer bet to speculate against money and for goods.

Conventional wisdom in investing is geared to passivity, not toward monetary fluctuations. Since 1965, that kind of thinking has been loss-producing. We want to take something for granted in our equations, and money has been our chosen stable factor. But our government's policies have been opposed to stable money. The familiar monetary unit is a thing of the past. We must all be active speculators. We must speculate in the knowledge that trustworthy money is a thing of the past. Passivity toward monetary affairs is not benign neglect; it is loss-producing. The government is actively inflating. We must be actively evading.

Conclusion

If you want to avoid turkeys, start with the dollar.

10

EXPLOITATION AND KNOWLEDGE

The profit motive: everyone knows that the free market economic system operates in terms of the profit motive. The trouble is, hardly anyone understands where profits come from. This includes businessmen who make them. This failure to understand the source of profits has given a real advantage to the critics of the market. When the supposed defenders of the market argue that the hope for profit is the motivating force of capitalism, yet they cannot state clearly where profits come from, they have left themselves intellectually defenseless.

The critics claim that profits come from the ability of the stronger, richer, and more ruthless members of the society to exploit their weaker neighbors. The word "exploitation" has been a favorite one in socialist circles. Marx made the word a weapon against capitalism. The workers are exploited by the capitalists, Marx said, because the capitalists can extract surplus value from laborers. The laborer has to work, say, three hours in order to have enough money to buy minimum food and shelter, but the capitalist keeps him on the job many hours longer. Thus, the capitalist "exploits" extra money from his workers.

The theory was absolutely wrong, and it was demolished by the Austrian economist, Eugen von Böhm-Bawerk, before Marx died.[1] Workers are paid the value of their output, or very close to it. When they are not paid according to the value of their output, other profit-seeking employers start offering them more, since they want the "surplus value" for themselves. The market price of the formerly "exploited" labor services climbs, since no capitalist wants to allow his competitors the advantage of hiring underpriced labor services.

---

1. *The Exploitation Theory of Socialism-Communism* by Eugen von Böhm-Bawerk. An extract from *Capital and Interest*. Libertarian Press, Spring Mills, PA.

Capitalists may well be greedy; this is the best assurance for workers that they are being paid what they are worth.

The Ignorance Factor

It might be argued that laborers really do not know what their labor services are worth on the free market. Therefore, they refuse to take a chance and threaten to quit. They are afraid of losing their jobs, and they are not aware of the better opportunities available to them elsewhere.

This is quite true; *accurate information is not a free good.* It is, perhaps more than any other scarce economic resource, the most valuable of assets. If men are unaware of an opportunity, then they cannot take advantage of it. But all men do not need to be informed of the existence of higher wages, or better working conditions, or jobs that offer more days of paid vacation per year. A few workers are sufficient to alert all the others. "Say, did you hear that XYZ Widgets has raised their pay scale 25 per cent?" That story, if true, is all that is needed to alert workers. The information comes to a few. They start quitting. Others wonder why their old friends are leaving the job. Nothing spreads faster than information about opportunities. Rumors are an efficient means of spreading information; in fact, the problem facing the listener is to sort out false from true information. But there is an economic incentive for laborers to check out rumors of major employment opportunities.

Consider a particular worker. For the sake of the argument, let us assume that he is indeed "exploited." His employer knows that he is worth, say, $10 per hour. But we will not call them dollars, since inflation tends to make dollar-denominated arguments look silly after a few years, or at least very old-fashioned. So we will not pay him in dollars. We will pay him in a hypothetical currency unit, shekels. (A shekel in ancient Israel was a unit of weight, which made it easier for people to know what units they were dealing with: shekels of silver, shekels of gold, etc.) The employer is paying him only eight shekels per hour, and the company is pocketing the extra two shekels. Or maybe the company is only pocketing one shekel, but charging less for the product, and is thereby underbidding the competition and increasing its share of the market. Whatever the case happens to be, the laborer is not receiving the value of his output.

What Can He Do?

What can he do to better himself? He can start investing. He starts putting time and effort into a "new company," himself. He starts investing in a search for information. He looks in the classified ad columns of his newpaper to see what other corporations are paying for labor services like his. He starts calling old friends on the phone, asking them what conditions are like at ABC Widgets, Inc. He starts calling the personnel offices of rival companies. Sooner or later, if he is really being exploited, he may find proof of the exploitation: some firm that is offering more than eight shekels per hour for labor services like his.

This investment involves sacrifice. When he searches for better information concerning the market he is participating in, he is an investor. He is a kind of capitalist. More important, he becomes an entrepreneur. He *thinks* there is a better opportunity around. He *hopes* he can find it by investing time and effort into his search. He *expects* to better himself if he discovers higher pay, or better working conditions, being offered by another company. He *wants* to take advantage of any such offer. But the key fact is this: *initially, he does not know for certain*.

If he knew for sure, he would not have to spend time searching. He would simply take the better offer. There is ignorance involved. He may not be exploited after all. Perhaps his employer is paying him a market wage. In fact, perhaps the market is about to drop; his employer may be paying him too much, by mistake. Also, even if a better offer is ready and waiting, he may not find it in time. He may never find it at all. There is no way for him to be sure just what the market is offering to people who sell services comparable to his. And even if he finds a better deal, he may not be able to convince the prospective employer that he, as a skilled worker, actually possesses the qualifications. After all, the prospective employer really is not certain just who this prospective employee is, or what he can do on the job. *The ignorance factor is inescapable.*

The worker who begins a search to better his position is, in fact, an *entrepreneur*. He is making a forecast: with work, and time, and telephone calls, he thinks he can find a better opportunity. He cannot be certain, but he thinks so. He faces an *uncertain future*. He is not omniscient. No person is omniscient. Nevertheless, he "senses" that there are better opportunities available. He is willing to invest time in the search. He skips Saturday afternoon television in order to find a better opportunity. He skips bowling with the boys. He skips an afternoon of fishing. In other words, *he invests a scarce resource — leisure — by forfeiting it*. He tries to get a return on his investment: money, or working conditions, or a job that offers possibilities of advancement, that will be more valuable to him in the *future* than the leisure time activities are valuable to him in the present.

Is He Exploited?

Is the worker really exploited? How has his present employer exploited him? Only by not giving him a gift, namely, the precious gift of accurate knowledge. He has not come to the worker and said to him, "Look, Charlie, I'm paying you eight shekels an hour, but ABC Widgets is paying at least ten per hour. I've known that for a long time. I feel guilty for not telling you. Now, if you want to call the personnel department at ABC Widgets, go ahead. See if you can get a job lined up there. If you do, come to me and tell me. Then I'll be forced to give you a raise. Fair enough? Have a nice day." How can we distinguish "exploitation" from a mere refusal to give away information that is economically detrimental to the income of the one who is giving it? (And how could we distinguish the *gift of information* from possible *stupidity* on the part of the company's management?)

Furthermore, how can we distinguish the worker who goes shopping for a better job from a capitalist? And if he finds the job, and refuses to run to all his fellow workers to tell them about the job down at ABC Widgets that pays 25 per cent more, how can we distinguish him from an exploiter of labor himself? After all, he has information that would help his buddies. He wants to take advantage of the information to increase his income. But that is precisely what his present employer is doing to him: taking advantage of better information. If there is only one job available at ten shekels per hour, and he takes advantage of it, has he become a selfish exploiter of his fellow man? If he forfeits the raise, despite his investment of time and effort in searching for a better deal for himself, has he acted rationally? Is rational action — taking advantage of the opportunity a man searches for — inevitably immoral, selfish, and exploitative?

Employer-Entrepreneur vs. Worker-Entrepreneur

How can we distinguish the worker from the employer? What is different about an employer-entrepreneur, who takes advantage of his access to information by refusing to give that information away, from a worker-entrepreneur, who takes advantage of his access to information by refusing to give that information away? The employer-entrepreneur spent years in establishing his business, and his profits stem from using accurate information wisely. He has *invested in information-gathering*, and it has finally paid off. He is beating his competition, since ABC Widgets does not know that there are workers available—or at least one worker available—who will work for slightly over eight shekels per hour. He is profiting at the expense of the competition: the other Widget company. He is also profiting from the worker's lack of knowledge. But if the worker finds out, then the worker is also profiting at the expense of the other workers (his competition) and his present employer, who now will have to pay him more, or do without his services. What is the difference?

The people who proclaim that capitalism exploits workers are really proclaiming something very, very different: capitalism allows people to take advantage of better information, at least until the competition finds out and starts taking advantage of it themselves. What the opponents of capitalism are really proclaiming is that men have a moral and legal obligation to *give away* the world's most valuable scarce economic resource: accurate, profitable knowledge. The critics expect men to give away a resource as if it were a free good, when we all know it is anything but a free good. It takes an *investment in an uncertain future* to gain ownership of this asset. Yet the critics want us to believe that it is exploitative to use it once we have discovered it. *The critics want to kill the private markets for information.*

Hidden Treasure

Some of the finest economic wisdom in history can be found in Jesus' parables. He aimed His parables at the average listener. He knew that they were not trained theologians. They would not respond to detailed theological analysis. So He went to them with parables, and several were "pocketbook parables." (Others were agricultural parables: seeds, growth, sowing, reaping.) His parable of the buried treasure was based on His understanding of the market's process of searching for information and using it to one's advantage: *Again, the kingdom of heaven is like unto treasure hid in a field; the which when a man hath found, he hideth, and for joy thereof goeth and selleth all that he hath, and buyeth that field* (Matthew 13:44).

Consider what the man in the parable was doing. He stumbles across an important piece of information. There is a valuable treasure hidden in a field. He is not sure just who it was who hid it, but it is there. He presumes that the person who hid it was not the present owner of the field. He is not certain of this at first, but he is willing to take a major step. He hides the treasure again, and goes out and sells everything that he owns. I suppose he did some preliminary investigating, just to see if the present owner will sell it. But the present owner may change his mind. Or he may have known about the treasure all the time, and he is luring the speculator into a disastrous decision. The discoverer cannot be certain. But he takes a chance. He sells everything, and goes to the owner with his money. He buys the field. Now he owns the treasure. He took advantage of special information: his knowledge of the existence of a treasure in a particular field. He took a risk when he sold everything that he owned to come up with the purchase price. Then he went back to the owner, thereby alerting the owner to a possible opportunity—the possibility that something valuable is connected to the field. Maybe it would be unwise to sell it after all. But finally he decides to sell. The entrepreneur—the man with the information and some venture capital—has closed the deal. He has attained his goal.

The Socialist View

The modern socialist would be outraged at this parable. The entrepreneur, who was striving to better his position, was clearly immoral. First, the land he was on should have been owned by the people, through the state. Second, he had no business being on the land without proper papers having been filed with the state in advance. Third, he should never have hidden the treasure again. It was the state's. Fourth, if it was not the property of the state, then he should have notified the private owner of the property. Fifth, failing this, he was immoral to make the offer to buy the property. He was stealing from the poor man who owned the property. Sixth, should he attempt to sell the treasure, the state ought to tax him at a minimum rate of 80 per cent. Seventh, if he refuses to sell, the state should impose a property tax, or a direct capital tax, to force him to sell.

What the socialist-redistributionist objects to is *the lack of mankind's omniscience*. The economy should operate as smoothly, as efficiently, and as profit-free as an economy in which all participants had equally good knowledge—perfect knowledge—as all other participants. Knowledge, in a "decent" social order, is a universally available free good, equally available to all, and equally acted upon by all. It is only the existence of private property, and personal greed, and a willingness to exploit the poor, that has created our world of scarcity, profits, and losses. Knowledge abut the future should be regarded as a free good. Profits are therefore evil, not to mention unnecessary, in a sound economy. This has been the argument—the real, underlying, implicit argument—of all those who equate profits and exploitation. Men are not God; they are not omniscient. This angers the socialists, and they strike out in wrath against the market order which seeks to encourage men to search for better information so that they can profit from its application in economic affairs. The socialists prefer to stop the search for information concerning the uncertain future, rather than to allow private citizens to profit personally from the use of knowledge in society.

The Transfer of Knowledge

Accurate knowledge of the future is a valuable asset. How can society profit from its discovery and application? Not everyone wants to take the time and trouble to search out the future. No one can take the time and trouble to search out *all* the possible bits of information concerning an uncertain future that might be useful to him or his family. So we allow others to do the work, bear the risk of action, and sell us the results at a price we are willing and able to pay. We consumers become the users, and therefore the beneficiaries, of the entrepreneur's willingness and ability to peer into the future, to take steps to meet the demand of the uncertain future, and to deliver the finished product—consumer goods, consumer services, or spiritual insights—at a price we are willing to pay. Why should we care what price he paid, or what risks he bore, when we pay the price? Sure, if we knew what he paid, we might guess that he is willing to take less than what he is asking, but why should we care from a *moral* standpoint what he paid versus what he is asking us to pay?

Besides, the existence of his profit on any transaction encourages other entrepreneurs to search out similar opportunities to present to us in the future. Let us consider our old friend, the entrepreneur-worker. He accepts the job with ABC Widgets. The other workers throw a farewell party for him. The conversation inevitably gets around to the reason why he is leaving. "Hey, Charlie, why are you leaving XYZ Widgets? Haven't we had great times together? What are you trying to do, get on their bowling team or something?" And Charlie may be willing to tell them why, now that he knows he has *his* job, and there are others just like it available. Now, he can look like a smart cookie in front of his friends. "I'm leaving because I'm going to make 25 per cent more each week, that's why. Why should I stay here at XYZ Widgets and work for less than I'm worth?" That bit of information will make itself felt in the labor market of XYZ Widgets very, very fast. The management of XYZ Widgets will have to do some explaining, and perhaps make some wage adjustments for the workers, as the effects of the new knowledge are felt. *The spread of information is rapid because the pay-off for those who have it is immediate, and personally beneficial for those who act in terms of it.*

A Chance to Profit from the Use of Better Knowledge

If knowledge is a scarce economic resource, and if it is a good thing for members of society to act in terms of accurate information, then it is certainly a wise policy to allow citizens to profit from the use of better knowledge. That way, there is an economic incentive for others to enter the "knowledge market" and take advantage of whatever knowledge is available. The spread of accurate knowledge is increased because of the profit potential offered to acting individuals. If better knowledge is a valuable asset, then its sale in the market should be encouraged.

Inaccurate knowledge should be dropped rapidly. How do we best stop the transfer of inaccurate knowledge? *Make it expensive to act in terms of inaccurate knowledge.* This is why we need opportunities to make losses as well as profits. Make the use of inaccurate knowledge expensive to those who use it, and you will discourage its transfer through the whole society. This is perhaps more important than encouraging the production or discovery of new, accurate knowledge. There are always more good ideas available than capital to finance them. But the continued use of bad ideas—loss-producing ideas—inhibits the build-up of capital. It is always very risky to launch a new project, since there are so many variables. But dropping a bad idea is an immediate benefit to society, for it increases the capital base—the information base—by removing a major source of capital consumption. The existence of *losses* testifies to the existence of *inappropriate plans* in an economy. Without negative feedback—the loss portion of the profit-and-loss sheet-society has no effective way to eliminate bad ideas. If men see the danger of establishing censorship boards to reduce the spread of knowledge, they had better cling to the free market's mechanism of eliminating resource-absorbing, erroneous information.

Conclusion

The word "exploitation" should be understood by those people who are likely to be the victims of true exploitation. Exploitation in a market order means the personally beneficial use of accurate economic information. Socialist programs to reduce exploitation are, in the final analysis, programs to make it unprofitable for forecasters to launch risky ventures based on their predictions concerning the uncertain future. These socialist programs are also based on a false view of knowledge: that it is a free good that is available to all, if only private ownership were abolished. By abolishing "exploitation"—the profitable use of knowledge—the socialists will inevitably *reduce the flow of accurate knowledge* of economic conditions. The public will have more inaccurate knowledge in its capital structure, and therefore more losses, with fewer profits to compensate for the losses. Men will not be the beneficiaries of uncertainty-bearing forecasters. The state becomes the active suppressor of the spread of accurate knowledge. If this is not exploitation, what is?

What we need is a means of reducing "exploitation"—the profitability of suppressing knowledge. The exploitation of another man's ignorance cannot long continue in a society in which there is freedom of expression, *if* this freedom is accompanied by the freedom to act on the information provided by the freedom of expression. It means that each man's "exploitation" of the resource of knowledge is always threatened by his competitor's "exploitation" of that same knowledge, as well as the "exploited" person's use of the knowledge. Knowledge is like any other asset: it is not a free good. Those who want it must pay for it.

The socialist brings a moral critique of profits: "Capitalists would try to reduce exploitation by making opportunities for exploitation available to all. They tell us that the spread of the legal right of exploiting others leads to a reduction of exploitation. Who can believe such nonsense? Exploitation should be made illegal. The best way to stop exploitation is to make it costly to be an exploiter." But this assumes always that knowledge is a free good. But it is a scarce good. So the best way to produce better knowledge—that is, the best way to *reduce the zones of ignorance* in a society by *increasing the flow of accurate knowledge*—is to give everyone who wants to be in the "discovery business" the right to get involved. The best way to obtain better knowledge is to make it profitable for people to increase the production of knowledge. By giving all men the right to sell all that they have and buy the fields of the world—if the sellers have the right to turn down the offer (i.e., have the right to keep "buying" their fields, day by day)—the hidden treasures of life will see the light of day. There is no treasure more precious than knowledge of the truth. That is why the kingdom of heaven is like a field in which a treasure is hidden. Give all men an incentive to search out the treasures of life. If we want more treasures, we had better encourage men to go out and look for them.

11

RETIREMENT

There is only one solid answer to the problems of retirement: don't retire. The only better one is to retire as a multi-millionaire, but it's a possibility limited to very few. Even Nelson Rockefeller said he didn't want to retire. He chose instead to return to the free enterprise system. (This amazed me; I hadn't been aware of the fact that he was ever in the free enterprise system.) All those who seem to be able to afford to retire want to stay on the job. This should tell us something. What it tells us is that it's nice to be on top.

It shouldn't surprise us that some aging coal miner wants to retire. Or that others who have physically difficult, or boring, dead-end jobs want to retire. The price inflation of the 1990s is not going to permit many people to retire in comfort, and virtually no one can do it without watching huge chunks of his capital blow away. The inflation tax is the retirement tax.

Nevertheless, the public still hasn't caught on. They continue to retire at age 65 or earlier, despite the Federal law which prohibits mandatory retirement at age 65. This ill-conceived law is one more example of bad results from good intentions. That the Federal government should intervene in the decisions of private businesses in this way is bad enough. The irony is that the age 65 retirement practice grew out of the old Social Security law. Paul Woodring of Western Washington State College investigated the origins of the practice and discovered that New Deal Brain Trusters assumed that Social Security would apply primarily to industrial workers. They didn't even bother to consult with those whom the law would immediately affect. They just arbitrarily picked 65 as the year to begin Social Security payments. Private industry picked up this figure from the government, and an American tradition was born. Now the bankrupt deficit in Social Security is looming, and the Federal government is trying to kill off the tradition the bureaucrats created. They want to raise retirement to age 68.

I am a great believer in continued labor, but I am strongly opposed to the new Federal law. On principle, it's a bad law. It is no business of the Federal government to monitor the polices of hiring and firing by private companies, state governments, or agencies other than those created by or part of the Federal government. What we will very likely discover is that the least productive, or least risk-oriented workers will cling to their jobs, lowering overall corporate productivity. One of the great restraints on Japanese productivity, especially in the domestic (as distinguished from export-oriented) firms is the burden of less efficient workers who cannot be fired. A company should be permitted to hire or fire as it sees fit. For large corporations that are already bureaucratic and increasingly inefficient, mandatory retirement is what enables them to recruit hard-driving, energetic younger men. Those men now will be tempted to join small firms, or to start their own companies, since the attrition rate will slow down in the larger firms. The benefits of free contract once offered to the corporate world are steadily being eroded.

The problem should be seen as one of philosophy, not legislation. What we have created is a national system of supposedly guaranteed living. Children get their benefits—education at State expense—while older people get theirs—retirement at State expense. People in the middle years are expected to pay. They, in turn, are supposedly benefited by a semi-monopoly, since both kids and older people are kept out of the labor force, which increases wages for those inside. It's a crazy-quilt system of redistribution. We simply refuse to allow the free market to operate. We refuse to let such factors as price competition and innovation prove to buyers the benefits involved. Instead we want certification: How old are you, how many degrees did you earn, how many exams have you passed, what color are you, what sex are you, and so forth? Bureaucracy begins to replace the market in a semi-medieval world of government protection. Everyone wants to know what his privileges are, not the market value of his productivity. "I'm 65, so you can't fire me." "I'm a minority group member, so you have to hire me." "I'm a token, and the government says you need me." One thing seems to escape the legislators: people can always say, "I'm productive and priced competitively; you'd be crazy not to hire me, but if you are, your profit-seeking competitor may not be."

The Golden Lure

The trap has been set; inflation is now about to spring it. What trap? The trap of third-party retirement planning. People have had faith in the competence of third-party experts. They have assumed that the Social Security system is solvent. They have assumed that their state or local pension fund has been fully funded. They have assumed that the trust department of the local bank—or even more foolishly, of some New York City bank—is staffed by competent, profit-seeking entrepreneurs who understand inflation, markets, and risk. (They do understand risk, so they have invented the "prudent investor rule" which enables them to waste most of their investors' capital in ways that will enable them, the trustees, to evade future legal action on the part of the sheared. They understand legal risk, and they put their clients' dollars into investments that are sure-fire losers during times of price inflation. Safety first, meaning their safety, is their motto.)

The logic of the pension is faulty. It assumes that individuals can transfer the responsibility of their futures to faceless, nameless boards of supposed experts, and that those faceless experts will put the interests of the investors first. It assumes that long-term credit positions can be taken in an almost irrevocable form—such as a corporate retirement program—without a loss of capital. It assumes that the best managers of one's retirement plans are third-party experts. This aura of expertise is deadly, for it lures the unsuspecting into a trap. It encourages them to believe what the market daily demonstrates to be false, namely, that retirement fund managers (or mutual fund managers, or bank trust department managers) can systematically and consistently outperform the market. They can't. Or if some of them can, it's random as to whether your firm has hired them rather than some outfit that consistently performs in a mediocre fashion. The odds are against your firm's picking an outfit which will be able to outperform the market for 40 years.

What are the realities of private retirement programs? As of 1983, about 36 million workers were "covered" (a most misleading term), down from 38 million workers in 1979. Not only were there fewer total workers covered, but the percentage of workers fell as well: 50.3% participated in pensions in 1983, as opposed to 55.1% in 1979. (American Association of Retired People).

Pension payouts represented grim comfort for the beneficiaries as well. Consider the following statistics:

Married	average annual payout (1982)
55-61	$4,700
62-64	3,990
65 +	3,160

Unmarried	
55-61	$2,990
62-64	3,050
65 +	1,880

The Changing Profiles in Pensions, 1982

1972 statistics show the average payout to have been $2,000 annually per beneficiary. (*Social Security Bulletin*, June, 1976).

This is a grim prospect for anyone who has made himself dependent on a private retirement program. What if the employer's program goes bankrupt? What about the loss of capital due to mass inflation, or a war, or a series of social disruptions?

The massive shift of personal responsibility has come in an era of increasing government intervention. Men have been encouraged to believe that some other institution will always enter the scene and correct any errors made by the inefficient or thoughtless. Government, or the corporation, or the Federal Reserve System will always solve the problems at hand. So people allow their employers to extract present dollars from them in exchange for depreciated future dollars. The government even gives people an income tax break to do this. (Not a tax break as such. The government doesn't offer tax breaks to the middle class. It offers only certain kinds of tax breaks, and virtually all of them are cancelled out by some future tax; income tax, estate tax, gift tax, or whatever. If the government offers a temporary tax break, it is only to allow the taxpayer time to accumulate more capital for later tax collection purposes. Forget this basic law of taxation, and you will fall for almost any sleight-of-hand tax dodge that the government can come up with this year. "Step right up, folks, and take advantage of this fantastic offer." "Put your pretax dollar under this little shell—uh, shelter—while we revise the tax code once again." And on and on.)

What must be understood from the beginning of a person's working career is this: a pension fund is a retirement program designed by a committee. Let this sink in. A corporate pension fund is something like a camel: a horse built by a committee. The committee selects its members in terms of proven, measurable criteria, such as an M.A. in finance from Stanford, or a B.A. in portfolio management from Harvard. People who shudder at the thought of the Trilateral Commission's running the country don't give second thought to the fact that their pension fund is being managed by people who graduated from the same schools, who bank at the same banks, and who read the same textbooks (Keynesian) as the members of the Trilateral Commission. (It occurs to me that Jimmy Carter was a President designed by a committee, and it showed.)

The thought of your future income's being determined by a committee that, by definition, believes in the "prudent investor rule," believes in the present-day "mixed economy," believes in the integrity of the banks, believes (or did right up to the end) in New York City bonds, and believes in the laws of Keynesian fiscal policy, should give you many sleepless nights. Yet the unsuspecting masses have slept soundly, knowing that their futures are in good hands with all-Statists.

A pension is a form of long-term credit. It permits a person to give up dollars of today's purchasing power in order to receive future dollars. Do you really believe that those future dollars will be greater in purchasing power? If not, manage your own retirement portfolio. Most important, keep it out of long-term credit instruments that are denominated in dollars.

What is true of the pension plan is doubly true of the irrevocable annuity. You give up dollars with present purchasing power in order to receive dollars with the purchasing power of 1990 or 2000. This seems to me to be the world's worst investment decision. Even if you buy a Swiss annuity, you are betting on the survival of the world economy, the investment acumen of the Swiss firm who sold you the annuity, the continued existence of a free Europe, and the continued existence of free flows of currency (out of Swiss francs and into dollars) on legal markets. Frankly, I would hesitate to bet my future in terms of these presuppositions. Deny any of them, and you ruin a Swiss annuity, and we may see all of them denied sometime during the next 20 years. (Still, I'd prefer a Swiss annuity to a domestic one denominated in U.S. currency.)

In any case, a person's decision to invest in a retirement program should be based on the assumption that he will never stop working. He wants the program as a supplement to regular income, which he does not intend to forego. He may decide to use the real estate management approach as his way of creating a new job for his supposed years of retirement, but he should never, ever become dependent upon passive income, especially passive income managed by a third party. That is suicidal, whether or not the government offers special income tax breaks to indulge in such suicidal tendencies. Inflation destroys passive income.

Does this mean a person shouldn't rely on the income derived from those second trust deeds? That's what it means. But what about those AAA-rated utility bonds (2010). AAA-rated by whom? In terms of what assumptions about the dollar, American society, and Keynesian economics? What about those other absolutely guaranteed credit certificates? That's the problem: they're absolutely guaranteed . . . in dollars. And who guarantees the dollar?

Two Steps to Take

The first and most important step a person can take is this: don't retire. Inflation will not let a person retire. He may not be able to work at his present job on a full-time basis, and he may not be able to do the work he likes most, but he must continue to work for as long as his faculties permit. His retirement income will inevitably be small and declining. Thus, it must be regarded as Social Security must be regarded: a minimal supplement to normal income, at best. A person who has to pay into a retirement program should accept the fact psychologically the way he accepts Social Security deductions: it's a tax that has to be paid. It's not a benefit, it's a tax. It's not a guarantee for the future; it's a drain on present resources. It probably has to be paid, but it's no blessing.

How to get out of your pension fund? Can you become an independent contractor? If so, perhaps you can quit, get your pension money, pay the taxes necessary, and start investing in something else. Then allow your ex-employer to hire you back.

Another approach: quit, take your money, and then get rehired by the same outfit even apart from independent contractor status. Sometimes it can be done, especially if you play straight with your employer and tell him the real reason you are quitting.

Can you start a moonlighting business? There are numerous books on this, like Don Dible's *Up Your Own Organization* and Peter Weaver's *You, Inc.* There are real tax breaks involved, namely, short-term tax deferrals, which are the best ones the government offers. Can you create a new company, or offer a service locally, that will supplement your income? Could it become a full-time job after retirement from your present job? If so, give it careful consideration. This could be the most important single economic decision you ever make.

I have never understood why teachers retire altogether from teaching. Why not start a private school? Why not continue in the profession? Why not demonstrate a little entrepreneurship?

The second consideration is geography. How high is the cost of living where you are? Most people are located in expensive urban centers because that's where the jobs are. But this means that they compete in a giant auction for the items in short supply, most notably living space. Why stay in a $100,000 home when you could sell it, move to a smaller town, and buy a decent $40,000 place, pocketing the difference (after taxes)? Or why not move to that small town now, establish the $100,000 place as a rental, and then get a tax-deferred exchange? You might wind up with a couple of nice duplexes that generate income in a safe place, and the government doesn't get a penny until you sell for money.

It is not easy to move. You will miss old friends. You will not be able to see them as often, see them grow poor, see inflation erode their savings, and take comfort from the fact that they're doing as poorly in the expensive city as you are. You may not see the grandkids as often, assuming your children are still in the same city where you are, and will be able to stay there in a time of turmoil. Of course, the grandkids might like to visit you on the farm. And your children might get their survival property in the only way they ever will, namely, because you have the vision, capital, and inclination to move out of the city now. But rationally, you have to move soon.

Should you move into a retirement community? Just what you need: the elephant burial ground for the white middle class. Congested streets, lots of old people complaining about their illnesses, lots of time for golf, puttering around, and being generally unproductive. Take yourself out of the land of the living, and focus your interests on the present, remove yourself from those who have a stake in the future. Hook up your future to those public utilities (water, power, sewage disposal) and pray for stable money. No thanks.

The Need for Income

Admittedly, if you're out of the work force and your skills are rusty, you may be trapped. If you have no energy, or your body is really handicapped, then what I've written won't do you much good. This is the horror of inflation: it strikes at those who are most defenseless. Yet it's standard operating procedure for every enlightened, Keynesian government in the West. This is the politics of envy come home to the generation that voted in its existence. This is the New Deal after 45 years, namely, the Raw Deal. This, frankly, is the revenge of the Invisible Hand.

There is a strategy which is generally overlooked. A person can buy a resource which he expects to rise in value and then sell off portions of it in future years, generating the income necessary for survival. For example, if you expect the value of gold to increase more than 10% or 12% per annum, you can buy small gold coins, store them, and sell them to the dealer from whom you purchased them. Or sell them to a local coin dealer. Or swap coins for goods.

This approach sounds strange. People hate to "touch their capital" when they spend money. Let me tell you right here and now, inflation will soon be touching everyone's paper money investments. Touching is not the right word; *grabbing* is closer to it. If you have a long-term, fixed-income investment, price inflation will wipe out your principal. So why not be smart? Substitute a hard asset like gold or silver coins, including numismatic (collectors) coins, for your long-term, fixed-income investment. You may see your capital increase even faster than the rate of price inflation.

But whether or not you choose the hard asset approach, your need for income will inevitably erode your capital if you cannot gain regular earned income. This is always the preferable approach. You should work as long as you can, while you can, and save your capital for emergencies, or for the day when you can't work, or for your heirs.

Longer Life

The Bible says, "six days shalt thou labor" each week. You will notice that it never mentions retirement. Caleb, who along with Joshua, was the only person of his generation who entered the Promised Land of Canaan, prided himself on his good health, and at age 85 he took as his heritage land which was more difficult to work (Joshua 14:6-12). He was not afraid of work. He regarded it as a blessing to be able to work as efficiently as younger men. This is the proper attitude to take. Good health is not an asset to be squandered away in meaningless leisure. Leisure's function is to refresh us, to re-create our energy (hence, "recreation"), to enable us to work harder, better, and longer after our time of refreshing.

One man who has led the fight against mandatory retirement is Millard Foist. Foist began a study of retired railroad workers, and he found some most interesting conclusions. Using statistics supplied by the American Association of Railroads, he found that the average life of retired railroad workers was about 2.5 years beyond the date of their retirement. However, retirees who began new careers added almost 20 years to their lives. Foist is convinced that the best thing a person can do after retirement is to start a new career. "New learning means new life and new health. It makes you more productive. A new career is something to look forward to. People hate to face retirement. They almost brace themselves as if they're going to fall off the face of the earth, and that's almost what they do. If you want them to be happy about changing, prepare them to develop a new career. So he went out and started a tool and die company, and he found that the older workers were more efficient than the younger ones. They were absent less, worked harder, had better reading and writing skills, and had more knowledge of their craft" (*Los Angeles Times* [Dec. 23, 1976]).

When people decide to start living, they will start working. When they are ready to die, they can retire. It is significant that the Social Security System penalizes those who continue working. Full benefits are not given to workers who earn over $8,160 a year until they reach age 70.

What most men need is a job to "retire into." It is important that they begin preparing for such a job several years before age 65. If it takes extra education, then pay for it. If it takes extra capital, use some of that Keogh or IRA money to get it. Cash in that retirement program. Invest it in yourself. Who better to invest it in?

If you really have some basic skills, would your present employer bankroll you after retirement? Have you ever asked? What if you had a project in mind, or a willingness to be a sales representative in an area not considered desirable or lucrative by the younger man with a family (or expensive tastes) to support? Would your boss see the advantage of putting some of the company's money into financing you after retirement on a strictly business deal? If not, why not? If he won't, how about the boss of the company's closest rival? The closer you are to age 65, the more carefully you had better consider this. If retirement is about to hit, or perhaps has already hit, I'd get on the phone and start calling up those ex-employers who might see how much you're still worth. Ask. The worst thing that could happen is that they will say "no." And there are often several people in a corporation who can be asked. All you have to show them is that you can earn more money for them than it will cost to put you or a rival in the field or on the job. Tell him you don't need the medical insurance coverage if he absolutely can't arrange it. You don't need the pension plan. All you need is the assignment, or some capital to work with, and a contract.

Can your hobby be converted into a source of income? Why not? Can't you at least teach people the skill of that hobby? Can you paint, clean up messes, repair broken things, babysit, teach kids how to read, or any of a thousand other projects? If not, why not? How much will it cost you to learn how? What about the adult education programs available locally? Can they help? While I'm typing this, there's an older gentleman rototilling my yard. He'll earn some cash for his efforts. I'll save time, so I can write. Everyone wins. Except, perhaps, the tax collector.

Conclusion

The secret of retirement income is retirement output. The secret of getting ahead is to compete. Col. Sanders started Kentucky Fried Chicken when he was a relatively poor old man. He died at age 90, a rich elder statesman of the fast food industry. Almost everyone can contribute something of value to others in the community, and usually whatever it is can be sold at a profit. There is too much to be done to waste skilled people's talents. If you can work, you should work. In any case, price inflation is going to make you work. If you don't, you'll eat up your capital and wind up a charity case. It's better to work than be a charity case.

12

RETHINKING RETIREMENT PROGRAMS

What is the proper approach to the question of retirement programs? This is a topic which divides the hard-money newsletter industry. I have normally opposed them. Mark Skousen, in contrast, has always promoted them. Why the difference of opinion? Is it the government itself? Is it the problem of retirement as such? Is it the safety of the programs?

The Reasons for Tax-Deferral

Whenever the Federal government grants citizens a tax break, we have to ask ourselves why. We are told that the government cannot balance its budget, yet the politicians are eager to get us into a retirement program. Why?

One reason is that the public really has pressured politicians to do it, primarily through profit-seeking intermediary pressure groups (retirement plan management firms). We all want to delay the day of reckoning.

Another reason is that the politicians are willing to defer a tax so long as they will *eventually* be able to collect it. It is a kind of "forced saving" by the government. They forgo the revenues this year in order to skim the funds at the point when you retire. The problem with this theory is that there is so little deferred gratification elsewhere in politics that it is difficult to imagine it here.

A third reason is that the IRS and Treasury bureaucrats (though probably not the politicians) see the potential benefits mid-term. They know that Americans are happy to declare anything, just so long as they get tax exemption. They will not think twice about the government's demand that they fill out forms, keep records free of charge, and limit themselves as to what they will invest in, if only the bureaucrats promise—cross their hearts and hope you die—that they will leave these retirement accounts sacrosanct.

By getting Americans to save more, the bureaucrats to some extent help the economy to boom (assuming that investment creates growth, in contrast to the Keynesian myth of consumer spending creating wealth). Interest rates might be kept lower, since entrepreneurs are presented with a larger supply of loanable funds, if the resulting Federal deficit (heavy borrowing) doesn't offset the increase.

But more to the point, the bureaucrats get their potential victims to put billions of dollars into easily monitored accounts that usually are managed by government-regulated third parties—firms that are ready to comply with government demands in order to reduce the threat of IRS investigations or other regulatory pressures on them.

When the size of this newly created pot of invested wealth gets large enough, the government can then sit back and wait for a scandal or two. Maybe some fund manager runs off with the funds. Maybe he invests in some crackpot scheme and loses most of the funds he managed. Maybe personally managed accounts are mismanaged by government standards. Maybe in the case of corporate retirement plans or long-term Keogh plans, the firm's owner mismanages the funds of his employees, and the government can highlight such mismanagement.

The government then creates a new series of debt instruments, "Guaranteed Retirement Bonds." These bonds are bought with maturities that equal the number of years remaining on each worker's expected retirement (to age 59, or 62, or 65). Then the government issues new regulations: each tax-deferred retirement plan manager must invest 25%, then 30%, or even 40% of the funds in these guaranteed, fixed-interest bonds, for safety's sake. The government then skims off hundreds of billions of dollars of long-term notes, which hardly anyone is buying any more. (The average length of maturity of Federal debt is about 50 months.) The bureaucrats thereby get access to the money, and yet avoid outcries, since the psychology of resistance is lowered to such confiscation. After all, New York City unions consented a decade ago to the union pension funds buying New York's "Big MAC" bonds in order to save the City from legal bankruptcy.

It is this psychology of deferral which is crucial. People want *immediate tax relief*, yet they are only marginally concerned with *distant returns*. Wealthy people would not put so much money into "tax shelters" if this were not the case. Avoiding immediate pain is high on everyone's list; avoiding distant losses is far lower.

"A Way Out"

A lot of voters keep hoping that the deficit will somehow be reduced without a crisis or higher taxes, yet without major spending cuts in their personal pet projects. So they think to themselves, "Well, maybe things will get better later on. Maybe tax rates will be a lot lower when I retire. If I can defer getting hit with today's high rates, and we can get Congress to back off later on, then I will wind up with more money when I retire."

It might be true. Maybe there will be some way to achieve this miracle. Also, maybe there will be a collapse, and your personal retirement fund somehow survives, and a gold standard is restored, and then deflation hits, and tax rates are lowered, and you "cash out" with lots of real wealth, untaxed. Maybe. Probably not.

But people keep hoping. A tax deferred could become a tax avoided. In any case, it defers the pain of paying immediate, visible taxes. People are willing to take tremendous risks in order to achieve this.

Will there be a way out before the confiscation plans — long-term Federal retirement bonds — are imposed? Will your personal retirement portfolio survive the crisis, and still be there, *purchasing power fully intact*, for you to prosper when you are least able to defend yourself? Will *you* find a way out?

My suggestion is this: *don't open a retirement program, until you have a* **plan** *for avoiding the pitfalls, especially* **official emergency political pitfalls**, *that today's deferred tax retirement programs offer you.*

Here is what you need to ask yourself, minimum:

1. How many years until I think I will retire?
2. What is my goal for the *after-tax* retirement capital base?
3. What could I do with the after-tax money instead?
4. How much will I have to contribute per year, given
5. What rate of return I expect to get?
6. Will I be totally dependent on this nest egg?
7. Will I retire into an inflationary or deflationary world?
8. Will I retire into a controls-produced shortage economy?
9. How flexible will the program be?
10. Who will make the major and minor investment decisions?
11. Will others be covered by the program?
12. What will my legal liabilities be to these others?
13. Do I really want these liabilities?

14. Will the bureaucrats change the rules?
15. What will the penalties be for *premature liquidation?*
16. What criteria should I use to *liquidate the program?*
17. Will my psychology allow me to pay the penalty?
18. Will it become illegal to liquidate the programs?

Premature Liquidation

I offer this rule as the foundation for any government-approved, tax-deferred retirement program: *assume in advance that you will liquidate it before you retire.* Now, if you are age 55 or more, you have no big problem. You are allowed to liquidate a Keogh or IRA at age 59½ without paying a penalty. They are unlikely to change this rule. If they do, liquidate immediately and pay the penalty.

I don't think they will go from the present 10% penalty to "illegal to liquidate" overnight. The bureaucrats understand that the real inhibiting factor is that 50% of ordinary income that you will have to pay, not the paltry 10%. If this factor were not strong, people would not go into these programs in the first place.

To brace yourself, you need a psychological ploy. Here is my recommended ploy: *always mentally reduce the equity in your fund by the amount of tax you would have to pay.* You don't have $25,000 in the fund, you have $15,000, or whatever you would have left over after the tax bite of your ordinary income bracket. *Learn to think this way.*

Then you tack on the 10% penalty, or whatever it is raised to, and assess the damage of premature liquidation. But you must always *discount the capital base by the liquidation costs.* If you don't, the bureaucrats will probably suck you in "for just a few years more." They will get your money, and then increase the penalty for early retirement.

Want to know what I really think will happen? The worst-case scenario? A demagogue gets into office and pushes an emergency order (which Congress will not override) which deposits all these funds into the Social Security system, for everyone who has a net worth (not counting home ownership) of [$]. Fill in the blank with whatever the tyrant thinks he can get away with. We could see an envy-grab of whatever retirement programs of the upper middle class.

As I said before, I don't think this will be done overnight. There will have to be a major crisis for any President to risk this sort of emergency action. But it is during such emergency-type conditions that you need access to your funds; they should be liquidated before the Federal government's fiscal crisis gets so bad that some tyrant is willing to take such a risk.

The time to start thinking about a premature liquidation is when a new President is elected on a radical platform, probably with a shift in Presidential political parties, and with both houses of the new Congress belonging to his party. Alternatively, after a President is assassinated, or after he resigns in the midst of a fiscal or monetary crisis. In the first case, liquidate at least by the week preceding his inauguration. In the second case, liquidate a few days after the newly inaugurated President's reassuring addresses to the nation have sent the stock market up 30 or 40 points from the assassination or resignation low point, but before he gets around to rewriting the tax code.

Another time to start thinking about it is when the price of gold goes over $1,500 per ounce, in response to three or four near-bankruptcies of major oil companies, banks, or Fortune 500 corporations.

If you start reading about major scandals in managing retirement programs, start getting ready to liquidate. The orchestrated press will have to be whooped up in advance.

Never forget, Congress has the fattest retirement program in the land. They will not rely on corporate funds to tide them over, at least not those who have been re-elected three or four times. They take care of their own. They are not under Social Security. So whatever they do to the rest of us will not affect them.

Anyone who is not psychologically ready to liquidate, or who has no mental criteria to force his own hand, should not get into any retirement program more high powered than an IRA.

Serious Retirement

Will you really need money when you retire? In short, *do you really intend to retire?* Not if you're smart. Your number-one priority should be to create a home business into which you will "retire." You will simply shift the percentage of your time which is devoted to jobs A and B, with 100% of your work days going to job B. What I recommend is *retirement avoidance*.

I think there will be an increasing demand for independent contractors along the lines of "Kelly Girl" and "Manpower." I think it will pay entrepreneurs to set up firms that hire retired experts part time. I guess I might call it "Old Coots and Geezers, Inc." (If the

"Beach Boys" can still dodder up to the stage, grey beards, thinning hair, and all, why not the rest of us?)

Let me give you an example. My father is a retired FBI agent, Hoover era. He works part time for a very savvy firm, M.S.M. Security, Inc., of Lanham, Maryland, which figured out there was a bank deposit vault full of money lying around in the form of retired FBI agents and other retired professional investigators. The company started lining up retired agents all over the country. Then it went to the Department of Defense and offered to do the screening of high security placement personnel that the Air Force or other armed forces might want to hire or promote. The military's internal screening program, being bureaucratic, is comparatively slow and expensive. M.S.M. can cut the screening time by something like 60% to 70%, and cut the cost accordingly. It can sell this service profitably. This also frees up full-time military personnel for other jobs more closely associated with national defense. The company hires skilled retired agents who spent a career doing this sort of work, and pays them $15 an hour, plus travel expenses. These men are glad to get the supplementary income. The government retirement program at the moment is generous, so they don't have to be paid full-time professional wages. I see this sort of company springing up all over the place as the economy gets into crisis mode.

If you are a knowledgeable professional, there is no reason short of laziness, enormous wealth, or Alzheimer's disease that should prohibit you from staying in the work force at least a decade after retirement age. I think your first retirement strategy is to decide not to retire and plan accordingly. I think that the best tax shelter is starting up a business that provides tax-deferral opportunities as part of its basic structure. (Maybe you should get involved in multi-level marketing. Anything!)

If you can free yourself from the dark cloud of forced retirement, and therefore from the limitations of retirement income (capital consumption), you then can start talking about how to structure a tax-deferred retirement investment.

A Nest Egg Omelette

How should you look at your retirement program? As a nest egg (emergency fund)? As a way to get untaxed capital growth (the "miracle of compound growth")? As a way to get the money needed to fund an already operating small business after retirement? As a way to finance a real estate empire after retirement? What?

I have a distinctly unconventional approach to this question. I see a retirement fund as a dual fund: 1) mental back-up for higher-risk, investing today, or 2) as a high-risk capital growth vehicle for a person with good income possibilities.

Let me give you some examples. If you are willing to take Saturdays or week-nights for building up a family business over a ten year period (or more), then your retirement fund should be a high-compounding vehicle to supply you with "mental reserves." Your real goal is the growth of your second business. You need to develop the skills of business management, entrepreneurship, and all the other skills that go into operating an independent business. That retirement fund soothes your wife's fears. It also is *legally immune to bankruptcy proceedings*, should that grim possibility ever occur. You can say to her (or yourself): "If I fall on my nose with the second business, at least I will have reserves later on."

On the other hand, maybe you are a physician or other self-employed professional. Or maybe you can "take your job with you" when you retire. Maybe you are a consultant now. In this case, you don't really need to retire at age 65. You have a job with your retirement fund to take advantage of the tax-deferred status of the fund. You need fast capital growth, compounded. You need a solid chunk of it in high-risk, high-return speculative ventures, on the understanding that you could lose the whole thing, or 50% of it, if your guesses are wrong.

In both cases, *you need goals*. You need a much larger goal for your crap shoot, since only a large goal justifies the risks. But you need to be able to sit down at the end of each year and see if you're "on target." If you need 35% per year growth, see if you have achieved it. If not, are you willing to stick with the program on the assumption that you will hit 100% next year? But you need to re-evaluate it every year, and if you failed to meet your goal, you have to think about shifting to a lower goal (which I don't recommend), or change managers, or stick with it, but by raising the annual return that you're trying to achieve (because you didn't achieve it this year).

When price inflation soars again, you will need to re-evaluate your after-tax retirement-day capital base. It will have to be increased, and so will your per capita appreciation numbers.

An inexpensive ($50) business analyst hand-held calculator will tell you what you need to do. All you need is a calculator with compounding keys. MECA's "Managing Your Money" home finance computer program has these features built in. But you need to evaluate your retirement program's performance annually.

Dick Fabian, whose Telephone Switch approach averages over 20% per annum capital increases over five year periods, year after year, says that *it is the goal which is crucial, not the actual portfolio.* The man who does not have a specified goal by which he evaluates his performance, and by which he motivates his investment decisions, is an implicit loser. It is the goal, above all, which separates the winners from the losers. He harps on this continually: *no goal-no success.*

It is far easier to sit down and set goals with a retirement fund than with anything else. It is a strictly "dollars and cents" evaluation. A business has many side-effects, good and bad. It has psychological inducements. To evaluate the success of a business in terms of mere dollars is ridiculous, if it's your business. But a retirement program is cut and dried. You set it up in terms of a *supplemental strategy to your overall life plan.* As a supplemental capital base, it must be evaluated coldly. Has it increased according to the plan in each year? If not, why not? And what to do about it?

It is the formation of your long-term capital goal which takes the greatest concentration. You must be realistic. You need a contingency fund, of course, but for major emergencies, your retirement fund will not be sufficient. Don't expect it to be sufficient. The ultimate contingency fund is your children. If you become a total basket case, either your children or the state (ha, ha) will protect you. Your money will not survive a major catastrophe—not the way today's full-time professional medical care in a "rest home" eats up a budget, unless you have at least $500,000 in reserve, pulling 10% per annum. If your children aren't able to care for you, there's not much your nest egg will do after two or three years.

But on the assumption that you will still be functioning productively at age 80—and you should pace yourself on the assumption that you will be—then you need a goal for that retirement capital base. Get it down on paper before you open anything more grandiose than a simple IRA.

What I am trying to get across is that your tax-deferred retirement fund is strictly a *supplemental* program. If you expect it to support you in the future, you are probably making a mistake, *unless* 1) you have a lot of income that can be legally deferred, 2) you can continue to do this for well over a decade, 3) you make few investment

mistakes, 4) the government-approved markets for retirement programs stay solvent, 5) the government doesn't change the rules, and
6) you don't suffer a stroke or other major illness.

You have to decide what your tax-deferred retirement investment program is to supplement: 1) a long-term occupation from
which you need not retire, or 2) a higher-risk family business that
might work out as the long-term employment source that you had
better be looking for. Your program should compensate for your primary source of expected future income. If your expected future
earning source is high risk, the retirement program should be a high-
return but conventional program. If your future employment income stream is reasonably likely to continue after retirement, then
adopt a "go for broke" program.

Going For Broke

What you need is a high-risk investment portfolio, preferably
one managed by a skilled person who is willing to monitor your portfolio and get the big pay-off at least once between now and your retirement. It should be a portfolio which can be turned over twice a
year, but without fear of tax consequences. This is why retirement
programs are ideal. The taxes are deferred. The compounding can
take place a lot faster.

I think the ideal sort of investment would be high technology
issues or exploratory mining shares. At least half the portfolio should
be in these high-risk venture stocks. If we get into a high inflation
mode, the portfolio could triple or more in a year.

The best high-return, medium risk managed account I know of
that has potential for high returns in both boom times and recessions
is Gary Halbert's unique commodity futures fund. It presently invests its money with five successful commodity account managers,
but with this variation: their investment systems are different from
each other. Thus, if two of them have a bad month, the other three
should do well. The fund carries an 8% annual fee, including com-
missions, which should drop to 7% shortly. The minimum investment is $10,000, and they are set up to receive retirement funds and
trust money. The best aspect of a tax-deferred retirement fund is that
profits can be reinvested and compounded. Contact:

ATA Research/ProFutures Diversified Fund, LP
7515 Greenville Ave., Suite 903
Dallas, TX 75231
(800) 348-3601
(800) 441-9045 (Texas)

Now, there is an additional problem. Your Keogh plan must be opened to all your employees within three years after you set it up. But a high-risk plan is *not* what you want if there is any question of future legal liability. So you may need to structure your entire program in terms of the particular type of small business that you operate. You should consult with your tax attorney about the legal liability problems. He should advise you. I only bring up the problem. You do *not* want penny shares as a major component of any mutually shared Keogh program.

Remember that you can set up an IRA program in addition to a Keogh. In my view, every dime of it ought to be with Halbert's program. That's what I plan to do with my program. Now that I've found a commodity account manager I really trust, *and who is being monitored constantly by Halbert,* I'm willing to break my long-term rule against retirement accounts. But I'm only doing it to get compounding, on the assumption that I'll sell out during mass inflation, take the proceeds, and put the money into debt-free land or a small produce farm later on. In the meantime, I want him to buy and sell when necessary. I want my compounding; I'll worry about taxes later.

The Safe & Sane "Conventional" Way to Security

The trouble with conventional plans is that they produce conventional (interest rate) returns. What you want is safety, liquidity, and yield (Bill Donoghue's SLY). But you can get that with a conventional money-market fund. You want better returns than that.

There is a better way. Get Ralph Goldman to locate those money managers, in the U.S. who have produced growth rates of better than 25% per annum over the last seven years. Goldman has tracked their results, using publicly available data, and he monitors them continuously. In effect, *he has taken the "random walk" out of stock market investing.* These managers meet several criteria, one of the most important of which is that they not manage over $200 million in accounts. Another: no short sales. Another: no "leverage" (borrowed money). This is safe investing.

Normally, these men will not take accounts under $25,000. Many of them refuse to take accounts under $50,000. A few refuse to take accounts under $100,000. So I went to Ralph and offered him a deal. If I can get my subscribers to use him as a "retirement fund money distributor," could he get these men to drop their minimums down to $7,500 for Keogh retirement accounts? He went to several of them, and most of them have made this exception. Ralph has to field investors' questions, calm people down, and otherwise reduce the direct communications to the selected managers, but if he does this, they are willing to drop their minimums.

This is a really good deal, in my view. The Keogh plan is clearly being managed by a licensed professional. He, in turn, is using skilled money managers to make the specific recommendations. Their portfolios can be monitored through public reporting requirements. Thus, *from a legal liability standpoint, this approach is ideal.* Furthermore, Goldman will switch money to new advisors, if one starts falling behind. He will be able to split money among several managers (you can put up to $15,000 a year into a Keogh), thereby reducing your exposure. *I know of no better way to let another person manage your retirement money.* This is doubly true if you have employees who may want to join the program later on.

Ralph Goldman
530 Court St.
Muskogee, OK 74401
1-800-331-9757

Dick Fabian also handles Keogh accounts. Dick's track record is excellent over the years. He also publishes a newsletter to let you know how he views the market. I am confident that his management will give you that 20% per annum that you had better get in any "conventional" Keogh. Contact him at

Dick Fabian
P.O. Box 2538
Huntington Beach, CA 92647
1-714-898-2588

13

INVESTING BY AGE GROUPS

I'd like to give you some material which I've had in the back of my head for quite a while. I want to get across some information that will help people make fundamental investment decisions depending on their age bracket.

Few newsletters talk about age specific investing. I think the reason is fairly obvious. Most newsletters appeal to an audience that is probably somewhere in the range of 40 to 65 years old. With such a fairly narrow demographic spectrum, it's easier to write for the needs of only that particular age group.

I want to break the age distributions down into the following groups:

> 21 to 30
> 31 to 40
> 41 to 55
> 56 to 65
> 65 and over

By the time we're through, you should have some indication of my investment philosophy and how it applies to each of the various age groups. It's important to remember that people have various talents and different capital bases. So, I can only offer a kind of general survey. But after you listen to my analysis, you should have a better idea of the problems I think these various age groups are going to confront over the next 10 or 15 years, and you'll see what kind of strategies can be used to help each group to defend themselves.

Age 21-30

Let's begin with the years from 21 to 30. Here, of course, you have probably the least amount of investing going on. Younger people don't have a lot of capital. There is that wonderful line that appears in one of **Poor Richard's Almanacs** back in the late 18th century. Franklin said, "A child thinks that 20 dollars and 20 years can never be spent." There's an element of youth that still holds to that view. The assumption is that old age is a long way away, retirement is far off, and you don't really have to prepare early for retirement. Of course, it's obvious that philosophy is erroneous. The earlier you start on a capital base, the larger that base becomes at the time of retirement.

Some of you are aware of this if you have read my book, **The Last Train Out**. I do an analysis of what one dollar invested at 15% interest will bring in over a working lifetime. One dollar invested at about the age of 20 or 21 becomes over a thousand dollars, if a person lives into his 90s. A dollar saved can multiply in an exponential fashion, if invested properly, and if the returns are reinvested.

It really does make a difference when people begin to invest early. They have a tremendous advantage, because the longer you wait, the more impossible it becomes to catch up with the person who has systematically invested over a lifetime.

The key assets of the 21-30 age bracket should be obvious. Youth is the greatest. Youth means resilience. In other words, the young have the ability to come back from a crisis, respond effectively and overcome it. Even if you don't fully overcome it, at least, you have enough capital reserves in terms of your age and time left so that it doesn't finish you. So most of the time it isn't a life and death matter.

Another major advantage that you have is mobility, both in terms of occupation and geography. It's assumed that young people will move several times in a career, both geographically and in terms of employment. There's no stigma attached to this kind of movement. Even getting fired from a job when you're between the ages of 21 and 30 really doesn't overload you with some kind of incredible guilt burden or public stigma.

In addition, a young person doesn't know fully what his talents are, and he doesn't know what opportunities are available to him, so it takes time to get into the groove. Mobility is a tremendous advantage that the young person has, and it is recognized as an advantage by most of his elders.

Another advantage of youth we don't think much about is not being overloaded with the burden of past mistakes. Now there may have been some unfortunate choices, perhaps a marriage that was too young, or an academic career begun in a particular field that turns out not to be suitable or appealing. But educational disadvantages can be pretty easily overcome. Mistakes can still be compensated for, so the burden is fairly minimal.

Another factor which is hardly ever discussed is the wonderful race to "keep up with the Joneses." At this point, most of the Joneses are 21 to 30, and don't have much more money than the guy next door. So, you're not yet in competition at that age with somebody who has 20 years of working experience behind him. A kid can start out and live in an apartment or a small old fixer-upper type house, and nobody really thinks there is anything terribly wrong. If a person can avoid ever getting into that "keeping up with the Joneses" phase, he can invest his capital effectively and let it multiply from beginning to end far more effectively.

There are several liabilities, obviously, that this age group has. One, they have little experience. They just don't have enough time on the job or in life. Experience counts for a great deal, especially things like knowing the ropes in a corporate structure, or in how to send out a resume. It is obviously a distinct disadvantage not to have been in the labor force for 20 or 25 years, because your ability to get the kind of job you are really interested in, at a price that is really justified for your productivity, is practically nil.

Also, today there is a glutted market for workers. Since the baby boom bulge of workers is only now tapering off, people coming into the labor force are finding it difficult to get a job. This is especially true for young professionals.

Also, young physicians and dentists, unlike other people, may come out with a mountain of debt, arising, not only from their education, but for startup costs for their practice. These fields are also increasingly glutted.

The same overload applies for the young person with a Master of Business Administration behind him, and is especially true even for the young lawyer. Demographers (supposedly, people who know these things) are convinced that the age group which is either coming onto the market right now or has been working for five or six years faces one of the most difficult labor markets for their age bracket that any group has faced in a long, long time.

Another liability is lack of confidence. Lack of experience simply means they don't know what they are doing on the job. Everything is new and seems pretty confusing. They are not absolutely convinced that they are in the right career, and may be having the early marital problems that face a lot of couples. They are not disciplined in terms of operating independently from adult supervision, and probably are just not that ready to do so.

This is a real problem with investing, because young people do not know where to start. They don't know how much to save, and may think, "Why should I bother to save when I don't know what I am doing? Why should I spend a lot of time with this thing? I can start investing later in life when I am more alert to what good markets are and when I know how to make money."

Finally, their capital base is small, because they haven't been saving long enough. Even if they did save, the money was eaten up in getting an education.

Those are the assets and liabilities of youth.

Now how do you apply it in terms of a systematic investing program in the broader sense of investing? Assuming that a majority of your formal education is probably over as you come into the labor market, you now face a problem with the job.

What does a young man just starting out do to insure his position in that job? I think probably the most important thing to recognize is the existence of what Napoleon Hill has called, "The Extra-Mile Principle."

In an essay that he wrote decades ago, Hill discussed the young man who starts out in business and goes the extra mile for the company. He works later, gets there earlier, skips the lunch break, and is always on hand when a superior needs him, even if it is only to get coffee or some seemingly light weight activity. But he is proving to the immediate superior that he is a cut above the average employee. I not talking about time and a half. I mean working the extra hour or two hours and not getting paid for it at all.

Let me give you an example of one of my own life hats. When I started out at my first fulltime job with The Foundation for Economic Education, Leonard Read came to me with a little paperback on the first or second day. He wanted to know what was in that book and didn't have time to read it. Leonard knew that he had just hired me, and my time was worth a lot less than his time. Anyway, I came back to work that night and did about a two or three page summary and had it for him on his desk the next morning.

Now, I wasn't married at the time. I was energetic, and I can write pretty fast when I have to. So, Leonard had it on his desk the very next morning. He thanked me that he had it back. I can remember on several occasions overhearing him say, "Yes, and the very first time I gave him an assignment he had the whole thing reviewed the next morning." Now the reality was from that point on

I had a lot of leeway where I could coast. I think the young man who starts out in life understanding that your first impression really counts will go far. He will honor that "extra mile principle."

Now the second important aspect of the job is simple: you can get fired, or you can get blocked from advancement fairly early in the game. If you just aren't qualified for that particular slot, or if your superiors think you aren't, you simply won't rise.

Let me stress at this point something that's important for every age group: get a small home business going almost from day one. Sure, it's under capitalized, but you aren't making money for spending. You only use it as a means of building up a capital base. Weekend service businesses are very good, obviously. Evenings after work count for a lot. No matter how small or how trivial the job—even if it's only going out and mowing lawns for people or sharpening lawnmowers—even though you don't really make enough money to compensate yourself for the time—initially, this is where you get your skills, your capital base, and your name recognition. You get a degree of self-confidence that is based on something you have produced, and you produced something that testifies to your competence.

Now what do you look for in your primary job? Obviously you want to look for whether or not that job is going to make available any kind of retirement program or retirement benefits. Generally, students coming out of school are only worried about whether or not they are going to be able to afford a good apartment, or whether they will be able to get married. They are not usually that interested in the retirement program. That's reasonable because you're 40 or 45 years away from retirement.

Nevertheless, there are certain things you have to ask yourself with any retirement program. One thing is, will the company match any funds that you deposit into the program? If you put in a dollar, will they put in thirty or even fifty cents, if you are really fortunate?

I want you to pay attention to this important principle. Many times a company will start retirement programs simply to sell their own stock. I do believe that's a good way for you to build capital. So, buy up the stock in the company you're in when you're first starting out if, within a year or so, you are fairly confident that you will stay. If the company has a matching funds system, then it's a good program. If not, then I don't recommend it at any stage. But if they do match funds, sell the stock at a discount, or give you some sort of special deal, this is a great way to go for the first part of your investment program.

Secondly, does the firm allow you some kind of options? Sometimes, the retirement programs allow you, once a year, to switch in terms of the business cycle. They will have growth stocks, bonds, or corporate stock within the company, or sometimes a money market account. Again, you need to have some sense of where the trade cycle is. There are some periods when you want to be in growth stocks, and some periods when you want to be in a short-term money market fund. I don't think, except under the rarest of circumstances, you ever want to be in long-term bonds.

If they don't have a retirement program, you should think about setting up an Individual Retirement Account (IRA). I have always been very skeptical of these accounts. Primarily, I think of them for the young man as a way to sock away money for the moment. I feel that at some point, you will need to pull out that money and run with it before you actually retire. In other words, pay the tax, pay the penalty, take the money and run. It is the self-disciplined savings aspect of the IRA and the ability to defer the income taxes that really is most important. Perhaps when you're young and just starting out, it is worth getting an IRA, but only on the assumption that you almost certainly will pull the funds out of that account later on.

However, for my money, the best investment a young man can make, married or not, would be to purchase a small fixer-upper type house in a middle class neighborhood. Look for a house with three bedrooms and a bath, or bath and a half. This is purchased only in a crisis situation—not your crisis, but the seller's!

The approach you would use is the kind of thing that A. D. Kessler described in his book, *Fortune at Your Feet*, or in several books by Robert Allen. Basically, I'm describing the "nothing down" approach for buying small single-family dwellings.

The earlier you get into a discount house situation, even if you swell the debt, the better off you are. As this book goes to print, I think we are seeing the bottom in interest rates. If you want to get out of the debt six or seven years down the line, you can sell that house and probably make a considerable investment appreciation.

Many people have goals similar to what Jack Miller and others have described. You buy a house, then another the next year, another the next, and so on for 6 or 7 years. At the end of the seven-year period, you can begin to liquidate part of your housing empire to pay off one of the houses free and clear.

John Schaub puts out a very good course detailing this whole procedure called "Making it Big on Little Deals." It is one of the best introductory motivation courses I know of. It's expensive for a young person, $495, but it's the motivation that counts. If you have read Kessler's book, Schaub's course is extremely good. You can get information on it by writing Proserve, 1938 Ringling Blvd., Sarasota, Florida 33577.

You have to be reasonable in terms of what you want to do and what you want to achieve. I would say that the purchase of a house counts as an investment. By investment, I mean you aren't looking at this house as a means to pyramid yourself into a nicer, luxury house. Basically, you're living in it initially to save money, and so the mortgage payment and additional expenses are legitimate, investment expenses. However, when you move out don't try to move into a better house, but rather regard it as the beginning of a real estate empire.

One of the reasons I say this is because when people experience problems with a house, they'll want to fix it up and make it nice. When they live in it and own it, it is easier to discipline themselves to paint it, fix the sink, fix the toilet or do whatever needs to be done. Therefore, since it's an easier way to invest, living in the house and fixing it up can be a substitute for the normal 10% per pay check type of savings. Let me stress again, however: you are not looking to pyramid to nicer and nicer homes over a long period of time. Rather, you've bought a house strictly for investing which you live in only to save money in the short run.

This next aspect of an investment program is one I regard as the most important. I'm talking about your children's education. I believe you do not, under any circumstances, send a child into the public school system. You send them to a private school. If you want the child to get out of the jungle and out of the physical competition, then you have to enroll the child in a private school. I think there is hardly any long-term investment that can be made, dollar for dollar, year by year, that returns a higher rate of return than a good private education for children.

I would sacrifice, I would rent in the poorest part of town, if necessary, in order to get enough money together to get a private school education for my children. If you are living in an area in which there is no private school, I would suggest that it's time to get another job someplace else, even if you have to take a pay cut. That is true for children no matter what age group you are in.

Next, we need to talk about an area I have stressed time and again: life insurance. I will go into some detail here but it is applicable to most phases of a career.

First, price competition is important. Usually this means you buy an annual term policy (ART). You collect only if you die. Your premiums go up each year, although many policies allow you to revert back to cheaper, original rates, if you pass a qualifying physical examination.

Don't get cash value life insurance (also known as whole life), unless you find that the cost per thousand is as cheap for cash value as it is for term. I don't believe in decreasing term insurance either, except in the very specialized field of mortgage insurance. Normally, you're much better off with an ART policy.

If you wish to purchase an ART policy, I recommend the services of **Insurance Quote**. Stored in their computers are the cheapest, best ART policies from top insurance companies. All you need to do is take 5 minutes and tell them a bit of brief biographical information, and they'll give you a printout with five of the best, least expensive policies they can find. Simply call toll free (800) 223-9610. You can also write **Insurance Quote**, 1255 W. Baseline, #160, Mesa, AZ 85202. Ask for their **IQAnalysis.**

A very good policy is sold to non-smokers by the Old Line Life Insurance Company of Milwaukee, Wisconsin. A wife should not consider buying anything less than $250,000 on her husband's life. Half a million dollars is much better. This can cost as little as $500 a year in premiums for a 35-year-old male. MECA's computerized home finance program, "Andrew Tobias' Managing Your Money" (a very good program), has a personal life insurance estimator. This feature alone is worth the price. You can buy it for about $100 from 47th Street Photo in New York City; order by phone using Visa or MasterCard: 1-800-221-7774. You name your own financial goals for your surviving heirs; the program then tells you how much life insurance your wife should buy on your life, given the money you have said your heirs will need. I have never seen any husband under 45 years old come up less than $500,000.

In life insurance policies, the wife should own the policy with her own private checking account, and not from the joint checking account. The policy should be for a minimum of one hundred thousand dollars. Under no circumstances should she have less than that on her husband's life.

At this stage in your life, a trust is a very good thing to set up for the children. Generally, the trustee should be a guardian, in case both parents die. Both parents' wills should name the trust as the beneficiary for their life insurance policies. If necessary, you might even consider donating sufficient money each year into the trust which will enable the trustee to buy an independent policy for the beneficiary of the trust.

Normally, most people don't consider that young men are responsible for their parents in case they can't support themselves. Just in case something happens to him, the parents must have a policy on their son. At 21 or 22, it's usually not a problem. In many cases, at a later stage in life, parents become financially dependent upon the children. A very good way to take care of that obligation is to give the parent premium money every year. The parent then buys the life insurance policy on the son. If the son drops dead, then the parents become the beneficiaries. This gives them the capital base that they need for investment purposes. When they finally get to the point where they can't support themselves any longer, they are not cut off simply because there was a death in the family.

I also believe that husbands should buy coverage on wives. They are very difficult to replace. It is a very difficult, shocking thing when a wife dies, especially when there are young children involved. Policies should be owned by the husband, with the policy kept in a separate place. Do not put all papers into the same safety deposit box. The husband should have the papers relating to the wife in his safety deposit box and vice versa.

I believe that 10% of income should be tithed and 10% should be put into a permanent automatic savings program. The Skousens (see below) recommend that you have money deducted on a regular basis every month or at every pay period. Then you don't get used to spending it, and you don't actually have to sit down and write a check. At the very least, put it in some kind of passbook or thrift account made available by the bank. It is the regular saving of at least 10% of his income year after year, as painlessly as possible, which is probably the most important single step that a young person can take with respect to any kind of a long term capital base.

Of course, it is not as important as the independent education for the kids. That comes even before this program. However, second to that, this is the program you need to start early in a disciplined manner, and you make it as easy as possible to save. The government does it with withholdings for taxes and you should do it in exactly the same way.

You need a consistent savings or thrift program in addition to your normal retirement program. This is a separate, independent capital base. The best discussion of it that I have seen is in the book by Jo Ann and Mark Skousen, *Never Say Budget*. It is available from Dominion Press, P.O. Box 8204, Ft. Worth, TX 76124. It costs $12.95 and is worth three times that. It is very simple, very forthright, and very explanatory on how you set up a systematic lifelong savings program.

Now what about investments? What should you do? Additional education is probably a very good investment, but only do this after you know your job, because then you know what is going to be required of you in terms of better information and better skills. Only then do you put the money down. Start with a night school class, or a weekend class, or perhaps even knock off for 6 months or a year, build a capital base and spend it.

I think it is all right if you have to cut into savings to pay for education. It is one of the few things that I would recommend doing after you have built up some kind of savings account. That is a capital investment, and it usually gets very good returns. I would say that's one thing that you can do with the money. It doesn't mean a more formal education, but education related to your own field.

If you have to make a deal with your employer, do it. Go in and say, "Look, I want such and such education. I have discussed it with my superiors and my immediate supervisor. I really need the education and I will make a deal with you. I guarantee in writing that I will work for "X" number of years when I come back, but I want you to help finance this education for me."

A company president is probably going to do it. Especially if you have been with the company two, three, four years, and guarantee in writing that you will come back and work for him. Either that or repay the money within a period of two or three years. For example, it is an advantage to the military services when they send people to a military academy or pay for their education in upper-division through ROTC. If you have to make a deal with the employer to get the education that you need, then do it.

A non-conventional investment can be riskier at this age. Again,

I think real estate is one of the very best things you can do. Actually, however, you can afford to lose almost any kind of investment at this stage, because if you make a mistake, you have years to start over. I think that an investment should be seen as extremely long-term, not short-term. You don't want to touch that money. You want it to pay off thirty, forty years away. This is a very long-term process, and you have to think and invest long-term. You're after capital gains, not income.

Don't forget: the only function of income from an investment when you're 22 years old is to give you something to reinvest. My suggested areas are real estate, collectibles, (i.e., numismatics, antiques, stamps, or some area where you have a skill, and of course, the basic silver coins). Given most people's capital base, they can usually do only one of those things.

A good rule of thumb is to go where your skills are. If it is a buy, get it. Then regard it as a long-term investment. For most people, the collectibles would probably be better. If you are talking about a survival investment, it is the silver coins. However, if you're talking about the greatest return on an investment over a lifetime, it is almost certainly real estate. But it takes work, effort and skills which some people don't have.

Age 31-40

Now the next age group, the 31 to 40 crowd. What are their assets? The key asset shared with the previous group normally is health. That of course, is one of the most important assets a person can have at any stage in life. Obviously the next would be greater experience and that leads to greater self-confidence. You've got a more proven track record. You have a better idea of what you can do, and perhaps even more importantly, the people who make decisions in the corporate structure know what you are going to do and how you will do it.

They have seen you. They also have some sense of what your performance qualifications really are. You are mobile. You can move out of a particular geographical area. You can shift jobs or change careers and it is not so expensive. Psychologically, you are probably not as mobile as you were when you were 21 or 25, but you certainly have a lot of mobility and that should be used as a capital asset.

People should not stay in "dead-end" jobs that they don't like. Of course, I don't think you should do it at any age, but you certainly should not do it between 31 and 40. By the time you're 30, unless you have been in job after job as some kind of a job hopper, you have established yourself. It is clear that you have made responsible decisions as an adult. So when you make a shift, it's for your benefit. You have better judgment regarding your capabilities, and better judgment regarding what kind of options are available to you in terms of your career. It is an intelligent move and it should be taken.

Your children are still not in college, which means that they aren't quite to the place where they're bankrupting you. When they get into college, they will bankrupt you, probably, or come close to it. It's going to be a tremendous financial drain. But in that age normally, the kids are not in college.

There are at least some capital assets that you can put up. Also there are other kinds of investing. Again as in the younger age, you have years of investing ahead of you. A mistake will not kill you. You're in a position to rebound. Probably your superiors at work also trust you more; at least more than they would some kid off the street whose work habits and personal habits are not well known.

In the 31-40 age group, there is still time for corporate advancement. No one has put up any major barriers to you, so there's still a shot at getting ahead in that company or in that particular field.

Now what are the liabilities? One of the most dangerous of all liabilities in the 31-40 age group is the growing debt burden. There is a great temptation of course, and it starts much younger, but the great temptation as you finally begin to get some income is to start "keeping up with the Joneses." That means having external signs of success. People indebt themselves, especially for consumer goods, to a level that begins to reduce their mobility. They can't take chances with their investments. They can't take chances with their job. They are locked in very early, because they are burdened down with this personal responsibility to pay off mountains of debt, and it makes them much too cautious.

You should not be cautious ages 31-40. That of all times is the time for entrepreneurs to get into the habit of taking risks, calculated risks, of course. If you lose your ability to take risks and move forward at that stage, you are really asking for trouble. The older you get, the more habit patterns are established and the tougher it is to get out of them.

When you think about financial liabilities, a growing family is at the top of the list, if you think of it in one sense. If you are 35 years old, probably most of the kids are in school. If you are sending them to a private school, as you should be, it's going to be costing you a bundle.

Another major liability is the new phase in your career: if you're going to advance, you've got to make a run for it. You're getting to the stage where you've got to sprint, and the sprinting usually comes at the expense of family, outside hobbies, more important outside investing or outside reading. Most men lose their free time because they are pouring all of it into the business. And, as they prove themselves to be high-ranking corporate business material, they begin to cut corners everywhere else. That's the great temptation.

In my opinion, sprinting must be resisted at all costs. It's not that you should never go the extra mile or three, or never work late until 12 o'clock at night. But if the workaholic is ever going to establish very bad patterns, he does it between the ages of 31 and 40.

At some point, the corporation is going to slow down its rewards for you. That's simply life. It is important that you begin an outside investment program, in which you are doing your very best to get skills that are not directly related to the corporation.

At this age, you're usually paid quite well. Because you're competitive in the marketplace, you can leave the company. Corporations are competing for you, and they know you can take off or get into another line of work.

If you have been there 5 or 10 years, you are a pretty valuable asset. They need to compensate you accordingly, because you may fly the coop. However, the longer you are there, the less that is true. In the early phases of a career when the career is really established, there is the great temptation to give your all for the company. As a matter of fact, it's the other way around: the company should give its all for you at that phase, because it doesn't want you to leave. It is also going to work you to death, if you allow it to.

What about the job itself? If you are ever going to think about making a change, the late 30s probably is the time to make that decision. Don't forget: you are comparatively overpaid, and you can still make a decision to make an occupation change. Therefore, you're going to be in the "high bid" category, if a new company wants to pick you up. You have gotten good training at somebody else's expense. You have been on the farm team for several years. Your skills are a major capital asset. You are a highly valued item, and other companies will bid for you, because of the fact that you're still young enough to give another company 20, 25, or even 30 years of service. You must take advantage of that if you're going to make a move.

The next thing I recommend, if you haven't done it by the time you're 29 or 30, is to think seriously about starting some kind of home business. You have good, proven job skills combined with self-confidence, and you're probably not fighting for your job. If you don't want to do it at this stage, you're asking for trouble. You can probably afford it financially. Take time out of your conventional 9-5 business, and put it into an alternate.

Some people prefer to move on to a new company and increase their value that way. That's legitimate, but if it means having to play, "look at me, I'm a whiz kid" for the first 3 years to convince them they were smart in hiring you, forget it. Set up your own business, and prove to yourself and your wife that you're a whiz kid. Take less money, or even risk closing off part of your career to the company that is employing you. What you're after is long term.

Along with this, you need to decide at least by your late 30s, and absolutely by your early 40s, if it's time to get out, rather than up. If it's up, they have you. You're going to lose your mobility. Once you have lost your mobility, they can then stop advancing you so rapidly in order to lure you to stay with that company.

At that point, you need to think about geography. You are mobile, you have proven yourself, and you are a marketable item. Ask yourself, "Where do I want to live for the next 30 years? Where am I safest? Where do my kids have the best opportunities? Where is a good school? Where can I find somewhat comparable employment with similar working hours, along with the same kinds of responsibility, in an area that has a better future?"

I think that you need to think about choosing geography and sacrificing income, or at least salary income, by the time you're in your mid-30s. If you wait too long, you can't get out. Go when you can. The mid-30s is probably when you have the greatest mobility, in terms of demand for your skills, versus the kind of skills you are going to develop if you have to modify your career in order to fit into some new company or new calling. Look at an outside business of your own which is service oriented, especially if you're in the sales field. Learn something about purchasing if you're in sales. Learn something about repairs of the item that you sell. Consider servicing it. If you're already doing that as part of your job, then I think you might want to look for some other kind of business that will not conflict directly with the one you are already in.

Another important question is, "Can you get your children involved in the home business?" You can sacrifice a great deal of potential income, legitimately and wisely, for a less lucrative business if the children can be brought in early. That means the kids get work skills, respect for money, and they learn how to handle money. They learn about the responsibilities of business. That is so important for the children that it is worth sacrificing a good deal of income when you pick some sort of home business.

I am partial to mail order businesses. They have very good tax advantages. For example, let's say you are on a cash accounting basis and come to the end of the year. You've test-marketed some kind of a product or even some kind of service. Do a mail drop the last week of December, and all of your expenses are deductible in the year in which you make the drop. Then, because in most cases the months of January and February are very good months in terms of percentage responses on many items, you get the money back and you have another 11 or 12 months to decide what to do with the money. That is a way of capitalizing a business.

In addition, mail order businesses are very easy to capitalize and they're legal. Of course, you need to seek financial counsel before you start. Too, you can convert back to capital when you like: just don't do a mail drop at the end of the year; take your money out; pay your taxes, and go about your business.

At this stage in your life, it's not too early to start thinking about retirement planning. One of the questions you have to ask yourself is, "Can I collect my pension money in advance?" In other words, is that money invested? Can you walk away from the corporation you are working for and use that money, either to finance a new business venture or to make it possible for you to move? Will the money finance the move itself, or be available during the period that you're living in a new area? Can you get a deferred investment program? If you have been with the firm long enough, and you can collect your pension money, even though it may be invested, that money in your hand is a very good reason for walking away from a company. You put it into a more controllable investment program.

There's another question you have to ask yourself: Is your employer likely to remain solvent? The larger your corporate pension fund gets, the bigger the double whammy you face. Look at it this way: The more of your capital tied up in that pension fund, the more at risk you are if that business goes under. This is especially true if you have invested in the corporation's own stock.

In my opinion, if you have been on a matching purchase basis of corporate stock, and you have built up (over a period of 5, 10, or even 20 years) large amounts of the corporations stock by the time you are 40, you should convert at least half of that into other stocks, a money market telephone switch fund, or some other retirement investment option program the company makes available. It would be disastrous at the age of say 45 or 50 if the company went under, and the value of the stock that you bought went under simultaneously. It is much too risky, even if they match funds with you, to hold more than half of your assets beyond the age of 40 in your employer's corporate shares if you are a standard employee.

Now there is an exception to this: if you started the company, and you have half a million shares or 10 million shares or whatever.

One of the things you might want to do with that pension money is put it into a business. Let me warn you, however: make sure you run the business at least five years. Then you know all the pitfalls. If it survives that long, in all likelihood, that business is going to survive for the next 25 years. Most bankruptcies happen in the first 2 or 3 years of business, and the overwhelming majority in the first 5 years of business.

So the question is: Would it be smart to put your money into a new business? Is it smart to start out capital intensive? Answer: no, if you are just starting up. Make it knowledge intensive. But, if it's successful, you've had experience, and if a local bank loans the money to you based on your financial track record, then it would probably be safe to put your pension money into that business. Pay whatever taxes are required and any other penalties. But, put the remaining money into the business.

You are generally better off with your money in a home business than in a pension fund, especially if it is managed by a board of trustees. I think you will do better trusting in your own skills if they've been tested for 5 years.

You can also consider if it would it be advisable to start a pension fund in your own company instead. Start a Keogh fund or some other kind of professional corporation account, and manage it yourself.

Housing is another consideration this age bracket needs to deal with. By the time you are 30 or 35, you want to move up. Generally, I don't think it's a good idea. There may be exceptions, but, unless you are running out of space because you have a lot of children, I don't think it is wise to move into a much better neighborhood. That is "keeping up with the Joneses."

Most people are better off living in relatively conventional housing, a 3 bedroom, 2 bath type house. If you're in a decent middle class neighborhood with a house that is at least adequate for the size family you have, you are probably much better off buying a second 3 bedroom, 2 bath, house three or four blocks away. It will pay off much better in terms of making available money when you're retired. It is just not smart to keep moving up in houses.

My favorite example is a friend of mine. He finally decided he ought to move into a little better house, so he got into a fairly large one, maybe 2500 square feet or so. He owns 250 other houses, however, so having bought his first 250 houses, he decided he could live in a neighborhood that at least was suitable for somebody who was making say 32 or 33 thousand dollars a year. I like that sort of mentality.

I think most people are "house poor." While housing is a comparatively good investment, it's not as good as owning two or three income-producing properties.

One of the best things you can do is to decide to be satisfied with a comfortable house in a decent neighborhood, especially if that neighborhood is generally in the direction in which the growth of the city is headed. Invest your money there, and don't put it in the best section of town or even the second best section of town. I know it's difficult to understand that, but I regard someone who buys the very best house he can afford, not quite in the same light (but close!) to the person who buys the very best car that he can afford. That, of course, is utter stupidity in almost all cases. Buying the very best house you can afford is close to moronic.

You also need to consider the time involved in fixing up a home. The better you are in your business, the less time you should spend in fixing up your home. The payoff is not as good. But, if you are good at it, buy a home which you are capable of fixing up. You get much better returns. For every dollar you put into it, plus some sweat equity, you are probably getting two or three dollars of capital value back. That is a good investment.

Remember, owning a home is a form of savings. Don't mix savings with prestige! Unless you are in an extremely prestigious area, it rarely pays to buy prestige as an investment. If you are very, very rich, OK. If you have very high income, and you are getting tax breaks and so forth, maybe it pays. If you are in a sales field where you need to look good, OK, it's a capital investment. But that is not true of most salaried people. Every time you get a nice home, you are taking away from your investments, and I think it's unwise.

Next, you need to consider higher education for your children. This is a killer, financially. Depending on when you begin having children, it rapidly becomes apparent that you are going to have to shell out big bucks at some point. You have to ask yourself a whole series of questions: Is college financially necessary for the child in question? Is he at least a B + student? If not, why does he want to go to college? Unless he is in an extremely good prep school, or extremely good private school, why does he need college? What calling does he have, that he needs to go to college? He needs to know that.

I'm sure you're aware of the problems with most colleges and universities: ideological and financial ones, to name a few, to say nothing of all kinds of moral problems. And they aren't getting better. They are getting worse. I taught in them. I began teaching in the 1960s and taught through the very late 70s. Believe me, the problems are getting worse.

You always have the possibilities of the local junior college. Financially, that may be the better way to go. Stick with the JC for two years in order to save money. If not, it might be better to go into a local college, perhaps a private one. Your child can live at home and pay you some money for the use of his room, but not eat up the kind of capital that it usually takes to ship a kid away, to say nothing of bringing him home for all of the vacations. All of those things constitute needless economic expense, at least until your children have proven themselves.

What counts in the long run is: where did you go to school as an undergraduate in your last two years? Where did you graduate from? That is what they look at. It doesn't matter where you went your freshman and sophomore years. Unless your child gets a scholarship of some kind, normally it is wiser to keep him under wraps the first two years of school, watching the books, watching the friends, watching the lifestyle. And, of course, you might always consider a trade school or apprenticeship.

There are different ways of financing an education. My personal opinion is, the best way to finance a kid's education is to kick him out. When he's 20 years old, and it's time to put up all of the money, and he is off to junior level upper division work, boot him, cut him off at that point. Don't give him a nickel more.

Then, he can go to the scholarship department of the school and say, "Look, I am a B + (or A) student at a particular junior college, and I am willing to work. But my parents have kicked me out, and I don't have assets of my own. I can't go to school unless you give me a scholarship. My parents don't take me as a tax deduction any more. I'm out. Can you help?" If the kid is bright, industrious, and energetic, he can get himself some kind of financial aid. That's the way a kid should do it. At least, that is my thinking on it.

If there are special circumstances, forget that approach. Put up with the financing of it. But as a goal, it's not bad. If necessary, take the money that would have gone into education, and put it into some kind of trust fund which he'll receive at 25 or whatever. You could also just put it aside and agree to give it to him, or give it to him three years after graduation, when he is on his feet. In other words, give him the money when he has proven himself. In the meantime, he is legally independent, and much more likely to get financial assistance.

Life insurance in this age bracket needs to be increased. If you are over 30 years old and have 2 or 3 kids, you need at least $250,000 of life insurance. At today's rates, you can probably get it for anywhere from $300 to $400 a year. That money is basic, and it should be spent. Your heirs need the protection. This is the way you build an estate. If you drop dead, your heirs won't be penniless. I implore people in this age group to get at least a quarter of a million dollars of low cost life insurance. Fifty bucks a month will probably buy you more than this.

Let's look at general investments. The time factor is becoming more important, because you have fewer years to invest. It's important, but not absolutely crucial. Again, you have to ask yourself if a second business is your best investment. Is it time now to really begin investing more time in the second business? Consider, too, what I would call your advancement time within your profession.

Again, is real estate the best bet? It may or may not be. If you have real estate skills, you will probably make more money than any other way. If you don't have the necessary skills and you don't like real estate anyway, then you have to find some other kind of service-oriented business.

What assets do you have at this age? I am assuming that in the early years, you just didn't have any assets. If you have, say 10,000 dollars of investable assets, not counting the equity in the house you are living in, at this point you must get serious. I would say, you are buying protection against prices, inflation, catastrophes, war, price controls, rationing and so forth.

This is the time to do some wise investing. Consider putting 20% in pre-1965 silver dimes; 20% in small gold coins, such as, perhaps, Austrian 20 coronas, Mexican 20 pesos, or the small krugerrands, and perhaps 10% of that or $1000 in rare coins. If you can get them, I think it is wise to buy pre-1981 copper pennies. In case of a real catastrophe, $250 of those would come in mighty handy. Put 20% perhaps in a money market fund, and 10% in a so-called switch fund, if you are playing the market.

In other words, if you are trying to beat the market, your best way to do it is with a group of funds that enable you to buy and sell simply with a phone call to an 800 number. Now, if you don't have a savings program yet, in other words, if you don't have 10,000 dollars in reserve, you need to increase the pace of your savings. You'd better put at least 15% of your monthly income into savings if you can possibly discipline yourself to do it. Realistically, though, I would say maybe even as much as 20% at this age bracket needs to go into savings, because you have lost the first 10 or 15 years of productivity and you can't make it up, unless you are just a genius investor.

Now what about debt? Doesn't it tie you to the status quo? Doesn't it tie you to your present job, your present occupation, your present company, your present almost everything? It reduces your mobility at precisely the time you don't want that to happen. You want to take advantage of your mobility.

Debt also eats up your potential investment capital. An automobile debt is absolutely preposterous. That is the last thing you want to do. It would be much better to go to your friendly service station mechanic and say, "Be on the look out for a 3- or 4-year-old car that you've worked on that's in good running condition. You will make some money on the deal, but this is the kind of car I want. Call me when such a car comes in."

It is especially good if you can get a mechanic who has a good service trade with a clientele that is 50 or 60 years old. They don't drive their cars too much, and they want to replace them every 3 or 4 years. You can get a Buick or an Oldsmobile or something like that at a very good rate. You may have to wait for it. But the important thing to remember is, don't go into debt on an automobile. You've got to reduce your debt.

Age 41-55

What are the key assets of the next age group, the people between 41 and 55? You are at your highest level of security and advancement. In other words, you are very, very secure in your job if you have been there for 10 or 15 years. There are still advancement possibilities ahead of you. So, with the combination of security and advancement within that particular company, you are probably in your best position.

You're also almost certainly in your period of highest economic productivity, at least in a corporate setting. This is where, without killing yourself, without really scrambling or clawing your way to the top, you are in your best position to get maximum productivity out of your particular location within your corporation hierarchy. The reason ought to be clear. You have the experience, but you are still young enough to be energetic, do some reading, and advance in the field.

You are still in a position to be tapped into some sort of advanced management position. Now some aren't. Some people get locked into middle management by the time they are 40, but, at least there is the hope ahead of advancing.

In addition, your health is still in pretty good shape. Your mind is still sharp, and there are new avenues possible within the company. You have good experience, and you have a good-sized capital base, at least if you have been thrifty. Futhermore, mistakes still won't kill you.

There are liabilities in this age group. Although you may be in your period of highest earnings, you're also in your period of highest financial responsibility. You have kids going to college, and you have aged parents who may become a financial liability to you. So, your great income potential may be balanced by equally great responsibilities.

You obviously have reduced mobility. Beyond 43-45, you're not in heavy demand, unless you are a whiz kid. Now, if you are a corporate president, none of this is true, or if you are some super-duper advertising executive, it's not going to be true. If you are a really genius commodity investor, of course, you have been dead for three years by this time, so you are not really in the game anyway. But the fact of the matter is, at this point you have been paid to reduce your mobility. The golden manacles are on your wrists. Your company knows they have you, and they are going to steadily reduce your mobility. Now, there is still potential ahead. It's not that they have completely locked you out. But by the time you're in your later 40s, early 50s, well, they pretty well have you. They know they don't have to compete as heavily to keep you.

You have forfeited your great potential move by the late 40s unless you are very, very good. You then face another series of problems: boredom, and a lot of critical self-examination. By the time you're 50 years old, maybe by the time you're 45, you have come to the realization that you are not going to be elected President of the United States. That's out, and you can kiss it good-bye! Now you can sit around and figure out what else you are going to do with your life.

Your boredom is a threat to you, both in terms of your income investment and in terms of your health. At this point, you have really got to think about your most important financial need, which is probably a business to retire into. Time is now your priority resource. You are running out of it, and so it has a much higher price tag than before. You absolutely must consider retirement planning at this point.

Critical self-examination begins to eat at really successful guys at this age. What am I going to do with my life? Who am I? Where did I come from? Where am I going? That kind of question really begins to get at people and they crack up. Psychologists call it "mid-life crisis."

Often there are marital strains. Families begin to break up. There are only a few things worse for a capital base than a divorce. I guess nuclear war would be one possibility, or a major fire, or your company going bankrupt with your pension fund; but short of those sorts of things happening, there is nothing worse than a divorce. So, you need to see divorce as a very important potential aspect of your capital investment program.

By the time you're 40 or 45, inflation is not yet a total enemy to you. You can still make money by investing in inflation hedges such as leverage in real estate and so forth. Inflation is not a total enemy, but it is becoming one.

You know pretty well the company's survival prospects by this stage. At this point, you absolutely have to consider shifting your pension fund if you haven't already done so. Shift at least 50% of the pension fund out of corporate stocks in the company and into some other form of asset. In my opinion, unless you have tremendous inside information, it is much better to shift all of it out. By the time you are in this age bracket, all of your pension money should be moved out into other corporate stocks, a money market fund, or something other than your own company. It would almost kill you at this point—I mean you would almost never rebound—if the corporate shares went down, or the company went under altogether.

There is still little reason to move up in your housing, unless you have moved to such a high level in the corporation that it would be an embarrassment to stay in the neighborhood. Then it becomes a cost and should be understood as a capital investment to help you move up in the corporate hierarchy. They'd better pay you more than enough to make it worth your while.

At this point, though, you start putting money into small town property. One option is to consider being co-owners of housing with your children. One way to do this is to buy a house in an area where your children want to live. I'd suggest it not be the first house they walk into. It is usually better to let them live 2 or 3 years in a house of their own, if they can afford it, or in an apartment until they get sick of it. You may not want to buy into their first piece of property, but, at some point, you might want to go in with them. If they don't have any money, you buy the house. You get the depreciation, the tax benefits, whatever tax advantage you have, and you rent the house to them.

Sell them an option for, say, five or eight years down the pike. They'll have the right to buy the house from you for maybe 10% down and 25 years at a point or two above today's interest rate. They can pay you a thousand dollars down for the right to exercise that option 8 years down the pike, at slightly above what you paid for the house. That way, you get all of the tax benefits.

If your child is solid, and you presume that at this point he is solid, he exercises the option and pays you off, and locks in a future for himself at a reasonable rate. You get paid off in "worthless money" but you have transferred an important capital asset to the kid. Do this only at a time in his life when he is responsible.

What about college for daughters? Generally, I am against it, unless the girl has a very specific employment goal, and knows exactly where she needs to attend to get that education. The liberal arts colleges of this nation are just that: *liberal*. Their faculties try to pick off every student for humanism and liberalism. Daughters are especially vulnerable to this evil and highly effective strategy. I recommend keeping sons and daughters close to home until age 20, but especially daughters. Better to send them initially to a local junior college, since you can monitor what they are learning. If you spot ideological trouble, pull them out of school fast.

If she is determined to go away to school, but her primary goal is to get married to a man with a college education, then she can achieve this goal a lot easier and more profitably than by enrolling as a tuition-paying student. First, she should learn to type really fast.

This means she will be able to get permanent employment. A really fast typist can always get a job. The best way to type is to learn the Dvorak Simplified Keyboard (DSK) layout rather than the standard keyboard. Accutype translator and tutorial, a $40 computer program (819 W. 6th St., Winona, MN 55987), offers the Dvorak layout as a built-in alternative. Second, once she can type 80 words per minute for five hours straight, she can apply for a secretarial job at the college that she thinks she wants to attend as a student. At the very least, she can set up a profit-seeking typing service close to the campus. She can then find out if the school is really any good. She can meet people, attend campus events, and go to church nearby. She can save her money, and then, if she really wants to enroll, she can do so. She can make campus contacts first, which can help when it is time for scholarships.

Your time remaining for investments is limited. You must judge very carefully where the money goes, because you cannot make many mistakes. You need to become much more conservative in your investment policies. You start reducing your real estate debt. Ask yourself, "What kind of assets do I have now?" Say you have 25 thousand dollars or more in assets: say 20% in silver; 20% in the small gold coins; perhaps 10% in rare coins, maybe 15% or 20%, if you are good at it; maybe 500 dollars in your pre-1981 pennies; and if you want to do a little risk-oriented material, OK, 15% in a switch fund, 15% in penny mining shares, 10% in a money market fund and the remainder in a growth stock fund. You have no savings apart from your home. You must immediately begin an investment program with 20% to 25% of your income being saved every month. If necessary, reduce the money you're supporting your kids with.

If you haven't been wise in buying a home, sell out and get into a cheaper one. You most certainly do that if you are over 55, because you get the money tax free. In other words, you can take the profit you build up in that home and put it into a business or into another investment. It is much better, after the age of 55, to take the money and run as soon as you can. Get out of that nice home and that real nice neighborhood and let somebody else take it over. You take the money and run. Invest it somewhere else. Don't stay in an expensive house beyond age 55, if you can possibly avoid it.

Age 56-65

Now for the next age group: 56-65 years old. If your employer survives, you have high job security. You have a much larger capital base. You have reduced your debt if you have been wise. The kids are gone and your parents are probably dead. You may have even picked up an inheritance.

But now your liabilities increase. Your health is less secure. You are probably at the dead end period of your job. There will be no other major advances. You need to be very conservative in your investments, because mistakes can kill you. You are less likely to be able to make a fresh start, either occupationally, geographically, or in terms of your investments. You have reduced mobility. In other words, your chances of being rehired by some other firm are far less likely if your employer goes under. So your risks are increasing, and your assets may or may not compensate.

Now, you know at your age, you're probably not going to find a better job. Rare, rare it is, unless you are a senior executive, that you will ever find a better job between the ages 56-65. They don't have to compete for you. You are not going to make the switch. The executive ladder shuts down. You are just going through the motions more and more, unless you really love your work.

After the age of 60, escaping to a home business is high risk. That is why the mid-50s is when you need to start it. Your pay raises slow down compared to what they did when you were 40 or 45. The employers know that you are less marketable and they don't forget it. The company basically forgets about you, unless you are extremely good.

Now you face retirement planning. Inflation is becoming your enemy. You can't cash in on inflation if you are older and your alternatives are shrinking. Admittedly, the company is more stable. It may pay off your pension, if you have a pension independent of your own portfolio, as a more or less controlled investment. Maybe you are going to get a lot of paper money, too. Maybe the company will go under, but by this time you probably have spent your whole life with that company, and it will probably survive.

At this point, you better have at least 75% of whatever is in that pension fund in a money market fund option. Don't make mistakes. 25% should be in growth stocks. The older you are, though, the more of it should be in a straight money market fund.

If you haven't done it already, you will have to down-grade your housing if it is psychologically possible. If it isn't, then change your psychology and invest the difference tax-free, because the IRS gives you a tremendous benefit.

In this respect I always like to give the example of President Coolidge. He retired from the United States presidency and went back home. Home was a duplex, and he lived in it the rest of his life.

The other section of the duplex was rented out and was a source of income to him. Here was the former president of the United States living in a small place and getting income from the second half of the building. I think that is pretty impressive. If it is good enough for Coolidge, it is good enough for anybody, in my opinion.

All I can say about children's schooling at this stage is that you are free at last! That's one problem that has been taken care of.

Decrease your life insurance. It is getting expensive. If you own your own home, drop your coverage back to $100,000. That is probably sufficient, because you have your estate built up without insurance.

A major threat to you at this stage would be that your company goes under and that your pension and your job disappear simultaneously. The secondary threat is inflation plus price controls. That is, you may not be able to buy the goods that you need. A major catastrophe would be an illness, heart attack, cancer, or something of that nature.

Your number one asset is time in your second business. You must have it developed and operating by this stage.

Now what other assets do you have? If you have over $50,000, I would split it something like this: 20% silver, 20% small gold coins, 15% rare coins, again the old $500 in the copper pennies, and maybe 10% in penny gold mining shares. In other words, reduce your risk somewhat. Place 20% in a money market fund, and the remainder in a growth stock fund. If you have less than $50,000, you need to buy coins. You need to buy silver coins and gold coins and forget about the rest of it. Probably 25% of your income every month needs to be invested. That is the basic strategy for those people who are employed.

If you are 65 or older, your key assets should be zero debt and children that can help you in a crisis. You have a fairly large capital base built up and low, almost no housing cost, except for repairs and taxes. You have lots and lots of spare time. The Joneses that you tried all those years to keep up with are either dead or in a retirement home, so you don't have to worry about them anymore.

There are some key liabilities. Your health is failing, or at least, a much higher risk. Health insurance is difficult to buy. Job security is low, even if you have a job, which you may not. Inflation can and will eat away at your capital. You're going to face eventually reduced mental flexibility and low resiliency financially.

It is vitally important that you try to keep your old job. At the very least, try to keep the medical program. Reduce your hours to 30 hours a week, if that is what you have to do to bargain for your job. Shift departments if necessary, take a pay cut, but try to keep the job.

If none of that works, consider attempting to become an independent contractor. Take your pension money and put it into a money market fund, or something to back you up for your health care. The best retirement planning is to keep your job.

At this point, housing can be a duplex or some fairly minimal housing situation. Your money must be kept to keep you going. Life insurance probably should be dropped at this point, except for enough to bury you. Investment safety is crucial. You must work, if you can, and reinvest the earnings. At this point, the second business has got to pay for you. Now you can start taking the salary you have deferred and deferred as much as possible. Now you can start paying yourself a higher salary. Get your real estate empire out of debt. Get yourself completely out of debt in every area.

Now what assets do you have? If you have $50,000, I would say put 35% in durable consumer goods, 35% in gold and silver coins, 10% in the money market fund, $500 in copper pennies, and the remainder probably a money market fund that invests in foreign currencies. If you really want to be adventurous, keep it in a growth stock fund. It depends on what you want to do.

If you have less than $50,000 in assets except for your home, you need to keep working. If at all possible, take odd jobs. Save everything you can, and if worse comes to worse, become a consultant. If you have gray hair, maybe they will believe you.

The basic strategy, though, would be to stay working and stay on the job. Reinvest every single cent you can possibly get your hands on. Buy durable goods for a long time haul and then just use the goods as you can. The rest should go into gold and silver coins.

14

REDEEMING THE TIME

It is indicative of the present moral, political, and economic disruptions that the West faces that people are seriously asking this
question of themselves and of others who are supposed to know the
answer. Not that many people are seriously asking it, of course.
That kind of question is limited to those who have something to lose,
and who are convinced that the present drift of world events can lead
only to a situation which threatens everything they have built up
over the years. Thoughtful people who have both capital and a sense
of history are clearly in the minority in any period. They are no less
a minority today.

Nevertheless, the question seems to demand an answer. The
question is almost, though not always, rhetorical. It is prefaced with
some observations. They run along these lines: "The country is
going to the dogs. The government is getting bigger, stupider, and
fatter every day. We are getting taxed to death. People don't have a
sense of workmanship any more. The Protestant ethic is dead.
Everyone wants to get on the dole. It just can't go on like this forever.
How much time do you think we have?" Being a full-time predictor,
I answer a question with a question, a time-honored prophetic
response. "How much time do we have? To do *what?*"

Ultimately, the individual who asked the question has something
in mind, or more likely, a whole package of ideas. The problem is,
he has not sat down to think about what he is really asking. Time is a
resource. As I have said in other contexts, it is *the* resource. It is an
irreplaceable resource. You only go around once in life, as some
scholar has observed. (Or, in the immortal words of Hud, the cynical
anti-hero of the movie: "Nobody gets out of life alive.") If time is a resource, then we have responsibilities for the effective use of that resource. Just what is it that a person is trying to accomplish? Until he
asks that question and begins to answer it, the question, "How much
time do we have?" is meaningless.

What the person is implying is that he thinks that his capital, including his lifestyle, will run out on him before time does. The person really isn't asking about time. He is asking about his hopes and dreams concerning the time that he thinks he has remaining. When a starving man asks another starving man how much time they have left, they are really concerned about time. When an affluent man of the industrial West asks the question, he is talking about his familiar lifestyle, unless his most pressing concern is nuclear war. Few men have that as their most pressing concern.

Buying Back the Time

Time, like any other capital resource, can be used productively or squandered. If you consider the growth of television over the last three decades, you will get a picture of what wasted time is all about. Men all over the world seem baffled about what to do with leisure time. Never before in the history of man has so much "free" time been available to various cultures, and like sailors on shore leave, men have squandered their capital with a suicidal vengeance. In contrast to this vision of zero-cost time, consider the words of the apostle Paul:

See, then, that ye walk circumspectly, not as fools, but as wise redeeming the time, because the days are evil. Wherefore be ye not unwise, but understanding what the will of the Lord is (Ephesians 5:15-17).

The history of Western culture cannot be understood apart from an understanding of the implications of this message. The Industrial Revolution was a systematic attempt of capitalist entrepreneurs to redeem the time — not necessarily in a spiritual sense, but economically. The Protestant ethic, above all, was an attempt to deal with the limits of time, to see to it that it was not wasted. Protestant businessmen in the sixteenth and seventeenth centuries became convinced that thrift, hard work, foresight, rational calculation, and a close attentiveness to the ledgers would lead to a better, more productive world. This outlook permeated the West, even after the theology of the Puritans had faded. So when we look around us and lament the loss of that older vision, let us not be naive: the heart of its vision was the effective use of time.

Unquestionably, the West is in the process of erosion. We have lost our bearings even as we have lost time. The Marxists, with their distorted concept of linear time, borrowed from the Hebrew-Christian concept of linear (start-to-finish) time, are conquering the world in front of our eyes. Theirs is a sense of destiny, a sense of purpose, despite the fact that Marx's evolutionary universe was rigorously Darwinistic, that is, devoid of purpose. The purpose is now man's or more accurately, proletarian man's. Victory is inevitable. The Marxists seem to beat us in the world market place of ideas because of their optimism concerning the future. They are redeeming the time.

What is our conception of time? There are few questions more crucial to survival over the next twenty years. Just what is it that we expect to achieve over time? The West, which was once geared to the future, invested where its dreams were. It still does, which is why we are facing a looming capital shortage. Its dreams are in the present. "The future is now," coach George Allen said. As more and more Americans agree with him, we can expect rising interest rates, lower production, more demands for leisure time, more pressure for the four-day "work" week. Output per man hour is headed for the rocks, which means that our future income per capita is in jeopardy. This is one reason why I strongly recommend the purchase of high quality durable goods, especially tools.

The 1978 coal strike was a grim promise of things to come. They weren't debating over wages. They were debating about fringes, especially pensions. They were debating about future productivity, too, since someone has to pay for those pension benefits. Workers want raises now and a guaranteed income later on, when they retire completely. Other unions are likely to follow suit over the next few years. People simply expect income apart from present thrift (savings) and future productivity. The "English disease" is spreading fast. So is the English sense of time. It is the concept of time shared by the drunks described by Isaiah: "Come ye, say they, I will fetch wine, and we will fill ourselves with strong drink; and tomorrow shall be as this day, and much more abundant" (56:12).

The Reality of Crisis

The question, "How much time do we have?" seems to imply another: "What kind of crisis is coming?" It makes a lot of difference whether we have mass inflation, mass deflation, price controls and rationing, or direct expropriation of private property by the State. It makes a difference whether we have taxation through inflation, or property taxation, or income taxation, and in what proportions. It makes a difference whether the banks collapse or not. The time schedules involved are very different. Our strategy of planning will be very much affected by our choice of crisis, especially if we guess incorrectly.

By now, most of my readers know how I feel. I think the crisis, short of World War III, will consist of erosion, controls, rationing, black markets, steady reductions of per capita income, the destruction of pensions, bonds, mortgages, annuities, and all other forms of long-term credit. I think the crisis will last until the end of this century, at the very least. I see it as a transformation of Western culture. In short, my time frame is longer than most of those who are pessimistic about the economy in general. Nevertheless, just because my time perspective is longer, I in no way want to underestimate the magnitude of the crisis. When a nation's concept of morality shifts, its concept of property rights shifts with it. Our system of property rights has created the enormous wealth which we all enjoy. That enjoyment can not possibly remain widespread, if we see the alteration of the concept of the rights of private ownership.

What am I getting at? Simple: tinkering won't do it. No change in Presidents will do it. No technical solution will reverse the drift. No one-shot solution can possibly work. Please, for your own sanity and the preservation of your perspective, don't get on some cure-all band-wagon. That's what millions of Americans did in the 1930s, and we are witnessing the results today. It led away from the concept of personal responsibility for one's own conditions within a framework of political and economic freedom. Simple one-shot solutions are invariably tried by even simpler hot-shot politicians.

This is not to say that technical solutions can not help. In fact, I offer two. They are quite simple. They would not cost the public much. They would cost the politicians plenty. To get either or both into law, we would have to have a political revolution. First, abolish withholding taxes on all income (Dr. Milton Friedman's gift to us in the 1940s — streamlining government, ho, ho). Let's unstreamline government. Make everyone pay it all at one time. Taxes should hurt. Let people go into debt to pay. Let them know what government costs. No more "refunds" from the government. No more over-withholding, the government's way to force us to file annually (to get our money back, without interest). Second, establish tax day on the second Monday of November. We go to the polls on the second Tuesday of November. Have you every wondered why April is the month to pay? Wonder no longer. Minor technical revisions, right? Bounce it off your congressman sometime. Buy some gold coins while you're waiting for an answer.

I view our crisis as one similar to a man who is sliding down a very steep cliff, tearing his pants, digging in his heels, and praying for a handhold before he goes over the edge. Perhaps I should describe it this way: most people prefer not to acknowledge that the cliff lies before them. Some are already sliding down. Not many have gone over the precipice. But when controls go on, the bulk of the population will be pushed over the edge—not to fall straight to the bottom, but to begin that long, bloody slide down the steep incline. More and more will go over the edge, and these are the ones who will call for further Federal intervention. Further intervention will push still more people over the edge.

What I am looking for is almost universal fiscal bloodletting, but not a universal crash. (Again, I am discounting war, although war can not be ruled out. However, few of us will take the steps necessary to protect ourselves from nuclear war, so I don't spend much space discussing it.) A crash is conceivable, but we should go with the better odds. The ability of governments to create fiat money and impose "popular" solutions to price inflation must not be underestimated. In the international division of labor, the United States has begun to exercise its particular specialized skill in creating green paper with ink on it. Government may not do many things well, but it can print fiat money.

So when you wonder "how much time we have," think in these terms: How much time do I have to accomplish those ends that I have set for myself in each period of escalating crises? If I am correct in my analysis of the multiple levels of crisis, and the variations in each level, then each man should have separate plans for each period. He should have separate goals. He should have separate budgets, including a budget for his time.

Any man who is not setting up budgets for a future series of crises really does not take seriously the threat of those crises. The existence of a budget indicates a person's willingness to plan for a particular expected future. "No budget" is still a budget; it reflects a person's unwillingness to plan for the future, either through despair or unconcern. Again, we are called to redeem the time in terms of a vision of the future. The man without a budget has abdicated.

Budgets: What Is Available Today?

I recommend buying systematically those items that will be in short supply later on, but which are taken for granted by most buyers today. You should buy all those items that, in a panic wave of buying, you think you would be tempted to buy. I try to schedule my own buying in terms of future panic. I never want to be a buyer of anything—gold, coins, guns, ammunition, tools, toilet paper, gasoline, food—during a panic. Panic buying is an indicator of inefficient prior planning. I realize that anyone can forget some item, or not quite get around to buying it, but no one should be caught short in too many areas. This is why systematic budgeting is mandatory. A balanced program of buying and storing goods is sensible. Once you have one basic group of items, go on to the next; don't try to buy everything in each group all at once. Don't buy all your coins now, or all your tools, or whatever. Buy only those that are vital in the preliminary stages of a series of crises. There will be items available for an advanced stage after the preliminary crisis is noticeable. Never forget this fact: not everyone sees the future in the same way. The idea is to keep one or two stages ahead of the panic. It will always come in waves. Different communities will have different problems at different times. A housing shortage isn't hurting Louisiana much these days. Some future hurricane may eliminate 70% of New Orleans (the most vulnerable city to hurricane waves in the country), but New Jersey residents will not notice. You must prepare for the problems most likely in the community where you reside, or intend to reside, in the next stage of any crisis.

Today, we should be planning in terms of basic goods that are easily available. Bullion coins, a few weapons, ammunition (which will probably be controlled first, especially handgun ammo), dehydrated food, tools of your future expected trade, books on survival and crafts, and similar basic supplies should be purchased now. Once controls appear imminent, a person should step up his purchase of durable goods, such as a 3,500 or 4,500 watt generator (such as the Onan), spare parts, and more coins. Once controls are announced, it's time to buy a car, or at least get spare tires, plugs, etc. It would also pay to buy at least a small bit of ground at least 40 miles outside a major city, put a used (10 year-old) mobile home on it, sink a well, put in a septic tank, and keep the generator ready at home. This will be a major purchase. It is wise to have a credit line open, to get your land and a liveable shelter. The controls, once imposed, will inevitably create disruptions. You can hold off for a time, but when controls go on, fast action will be imperative.

Fact: you can't afford to do everything right now. The idea is to do a little each week, if possible. Get a proposed timetable, with warning signs, that you think will apply in your community. Get a budget outlined to fit each stage of the expected escalations of disruptions. Be systematic. Know what you're willing to give up at each stage in order to finance the purchases you will have to make. If you do this, even in a very simple outline, you are really serious about the possibility of government-created disruptions. A very simple beginning is your own self-testimony that you are doing your best to redeem the time, period by period.

Conclusion

How much time do we have? To do what? How much time do we have? To meet what kind of crisis? How much time do we have? To meet a crisis period of what duration? How much time do we have? To spend how much capital once we think we know the answers?

If someone told you, to the day, how much time "we" have, what would you do about it? Really and truly, what would you do differently? If the answer is "not much," then it really doesn't matter how much time we have as far as your budgeting is concerned. So the question is more of a curiosity than a piece of information in a program of crisis-evasion. Do you really want to know?

If you really want to know, then decide for yourself, once and for all, do you think it will be deflation (prices falling, so hold cash), inflation (prices rising, so hold precious metals), price controls (black market supplies, so hoard goods)? Do you think it will be a period of terrorism, or revolution, or intermittent breakdowns of public utilities (water, power, garbage collection)? Will it be martial law? Will it be rationing? Will it be world-war? What do you think the most likely scenario will be? Until you budget your time and capital in terms of one or more of these possible scenarios, you ultimately think it will be good times as usual.

Have you spent a weekend looking for a piece of ground? When you do, you will have taken a preliminary step towards preparing for a serious breakdown. You don't have to buy in a panic now, but have you at least looked? Have you bought a copy of Les Scher's *Finding and Buying Your Place in the Country*? These are simple steps. Use this for enjoyment but seriously spend a weekend just snooping around. Pick up a rural paper. So it costs you a weekend. So what? Don't assume that you will always have time to shop. It is time spend in advance planning that will keep you from gross mistakes. It's the assumption that you have unlimited time, meaning an unlimited guarantee on your present comfortable lifestyle, that can cost you too much gold or too much debt later on. If you're short on capital, you will have to spend time. If you're short on time, then don't begrudge the capital and the expensive mistakes.

Prepare for one stage at a time. And most important, have something productive in mind for you to do at each stage: productive when you're doing it as well as productive for the next stage. A man without a sense of meaning in his work is not a good candidate for long-term survival. Spend capital now in order to assure yourself that you will be productive and useful to others, in the market and in other spheres of life, in each stage of the long-term crises that confront us. Man does not live by protein powder alone.

15

RECAPTURING AMERICA BY THE YEAR 2000

I received a letter from a retired military man recently. He felt driven to make this comment: "I would like to pass along one comment from a friend with whom I share my copy of *Remnant Review*. He has recently asked me the question, 'Why does Gary North continue to live in America?' What he means is that you appear so negative toward the government of the United States that you almost come across as an anti-American. I think I know where you are coming from, but you do come across in a very condemnatory manner. Just thought I'd pass along my friend's observation."

This subscriber is in desperate need of some new friends. Now, how does someone respond to this all-too-familiar criticism? You better have your answer clear in your mind, because eventually, some sanctimonious compromiser is going to ask you the same stupid rhetorical question. If you continue to discuss what you read in newsletters, you're going to push someone too hard. And he's going to hit you with some version of "if you don't like New Deal socialism and its stolen goods the way we patriotic Americans do, why don't you just leave?"

Should Gen. Douglas MacArthur have moved from Korea and flown back to Australia in 1952 because of the things he said about the competence of the military strategy of the country? He was very negative, you may remember. He thought we ought to bomb the stuffings out of the Red Chinese. He found it difficult to understand why his civilian superiors had decided that his planes should bomb only the south half of the bridges across the Yalu River. Picky, picky, picky. "Why don't you go back to Australia, Mac, if you don't like a UN-controlled peace action?"

I think of my friend Gen. (retired) Al Knight. He is as eloquent a critic of Mutual Assured Destruction as you can find this side of Gen. (retired) Dan Graham. He thinks that President Reagan's leadership has been woefully weak. He has said so repeatedly in public. Reagan refuses to scrap MAD. Knight resigned his commission, as did Graham, over his lack of confidence in political decisions affecting the military. They now go around saying very mean things about the competence of the fellows who now are sitting comfortably in the Pentagon. (Read Edward Luttwak's *The Pentagon and the Art of War* if you really want an indication of how bad things are.) How's this? "If you don't like the Pentagon, you're clearly unpatriotic!"

How about this one for a Russian bumper sticker? "The Soviet Union: Love It or Leave It!" (Since only the Party faithful can have cars, it's a good one.) Or: "Since you hate Russia, Solzhenitsyn, why don't you go to the United States?" Well, he did; he was expelled. Why? Because he loved Russia; he hated only the Soviet Union, a revolutionary dictatorship that was imposed by force on Russia, and still is.

What my correspondent's friend is saying is clear: America is defined as the prevailing policies that the present political, bureaucratic, and banking rulers have created for the rest of us to live with. Furthermore, any continuing criticism of those leaders is unpleasant, bothersome, and basically unpatriotic.

Can You Oppose David Rockefeller and Still Love America?

So why don't I leave the country? An easy question to answer. Because I firmly believe that people who think like I do are about to recapture this country. That by the year 2000, political and market forces will have placed severe restrictions on the ability of highly placed elites to control events in the U.S. Therefore, now is not the time to turn tail and run. Now is also not the time to stop sticking it to the scoundrels who have made policy in this nation. Now is the time to shout even louder. In short, it's my belief that men of good courage don't stop criticizing incompetence and downright willful evil, just because a bunch of scalawags have taken over the reins of power (yes, including the U.S. Supreme Court).

When a free man can get 12 of his peers on a jury to say "not guilty," the Supreme Court can say nothing about it. The local jury is the ultimate legal sovereign, not the Supreme Court. The Supreme Court can reject or uphold convictions, but it has nothing to say about acquittals. That's what I like about America.

When I asked Gen. Knight during a Firestorm Chats interview

about the question of disloyalty to the President, he answered well: "I swore allegiance to the Constitution, not to the President." That's why he quit, and that's why he continues to speak out. He swore allegiance to the Constitution. Devotion to the Constitution is more important than devotion to those who have misused power by appealing to the basest instincts of the electorate.

But there are a lot of soft-headed people who think they are supremely patriotic by quietly submitting to Constitution-defying authoritarians who have taken away their freedoms (and mine). They resent it when others speak up and point out that a 70-year political rape has been going on. (Well, maybe not rape. Mutual seduction may be closer to it. "Soak the rich!" the envy-manipulators said in 1913, and the voters agreed, thereby sealing the fate of their children and grandchildren. Just because I worry about a kind of moral syphilis that has become epidemic politically and economically doesn't mean I don't love the country. I just don't like the pimps.)

The pimps lie, too. Red Beckman and Bill Benson (a retired Illinois revenue agent) have studied the history of the ratification of the Sixteenth Amendment, the income tax. Guess what they found? It was never legally ratified by the states. Washington knew it, too, but decided to let it pass anyway. See their book *The Law That Never Was* (Box 550, South Holland, IL 60473: Constitutional Research, Inc., 1985: $22). It's quite a story.

Now, is it unpatriotic to point to evidence that indicates that the government of the United States has been operating in terms of legalized theft for about seven decades? Beckman doesn't think so. Neither do I. But my correspondent's friend probably thinks we ought to move to Bermuda. "If they don't like paying income taxes the way everyone else does, let them move to a Caribbean tax haven!"

No, let us just get overtaxed Americans to abandon their confidence in the income tax in the U.S. and return to the tax system which the Founding Fathers established in the Constitution, which, legally speaking, was not changed in 1913.

I know, I know: the Founding Fathers just didn't know what they were talking about. The so-called Progressives in 1913 did. In 1913, it would have been: "Shut up, or ship out, Madison!" "Why don't you go back to England, Jefferson?"

Does this mean I recommend joining the tax revolt? My opinion is the same as Jesus': pay tribute while the Romans have the power to enforce tribute, but do everything possible to undermine people's confidence in the Romans.

We do this by replacing the State wherever possible. (Step one: get our children out of the public schools, or bribe our grown children with free tuition money to get our grandchildren out of the public schools. This beats any hard-money investment I know about.) We prepare ourselves for the bankruptcy of the State.

I have a question for you. If someone doesn't like what is going on today, must he therefore reject the U.S. Constitution? Must he also dislike America? That's what contented people will tell you. That's what people who don't want to work to reclaim this country from thieves will tell you. They never consider the alternative: "Yes, this is a great country, and we need to win it back from those who are hell-bent on destroying it." That's why these sanctimonious critics have become the unconscious agents of a conspiracy. Without them, the conspirators couldn't control anything. They need these "patriots."

The Conspirators

Want to get in a squabble on a panel discussion at any known "hard money" conference? Bring up the topic of a conspiracy. Harry Browne will ridicule you. Jim Davidson will ridicule you. I've seen it happen. Larry Abraham, the author of *Call It Conspiracy*, has been the brunt of the ridicule both times. People who haven't done their homework always resent the guy who gets his in on time and who gets an "A" on his paper. Just because these same people have done their homework quite well in their economics classics doesn't mean that they cracked a book let alone wrote a book—in history.

The evidence is clear. There is no excuse for not being informed. A loose-knit group of self-interested people have used domestic socialism to feather their own nests. They have created a government-protected monopoly for themselves. They have adopted as their operating principle: "That a sweet deal of the rulers, by the rulers, for the rulers shall not perish from the earth."

Dan Smoot was the first author to write a whole book about the Council on Foreign Relations, *The Invisible Government* (1961), 40 years after the creation of the C.F.R. It sold a million copies by mail order. His nationally syndicated T.V. program got him his market. I remember writing to him in 1961, telling him about a course in foreign relations that assigned several C.F.R. texts, including one by Henry Kissinger.

He blew the cover off the C.F.R. These days, that seems like a minor achievement. It wasn't in 1961. Five years later, Carroll Quigley's *Tragedy and Hope* (Macmillan, 1966) sneaked through the editorial board and sat ticking, like a time bomb, for over four years. That book presented the case, albeit an unfootnoted case — for the power of an English-based conspiracy that has directed the political affairs of this nation since 1913. The author was a professor of history at Georgetown University's School of Foreign Service.

For four years, *Tragedy and Hope* was ignored. Don Bell (of Don Bell Reports) stumbled across it in a bookstore in 1966, and reported on it. I heard about it through R. J. Rushdoony, who subscribed to Bell's letter. But nobody picked it up until 1970, when both Gary Allen and Cleon Skousen got a hold of it. Skousen wrote a book based on it, *The Naked Capitalist* (1971). It sold a million copies, 500,000 in the first two years. Allen and Abraham's *None Dare Call It Conspiracy* sold 4.5 million copies. The C.F.R. cover was blown, permanently. Their 50-year free ride was over.

And Quigley's book? How well did it do? Not that well; Macmillan destroyed the plates and refused to reprint it. The copy you can buy today is a "pirate" edition. The first "pirate" even had Macmillan's name on the spine. The later printings don't. They "pirated" it from Macmillan's suppressors, not Quigley, who gave them permission to reprint it before he died in 1977. It can be purchased from Dominion Press, P.O. Box 8204, Ft. Worth, TX 76124: $27. It is well worth it, if you're a history buff. Or a skeptic about conspiracies.

Can a book "sneak through" a company? A 1,300 page textbook sure can. I know of two cases where something similar happened. Otto Scott's remarkable history of the mid-nineteenth-century Unitarian ministers who financed John Brown's bloody raids, *The Secret Six*, was published in 1980 by Times Books, the subsidiary of the New York Times. Scott says that a senior man in the parent company expressed displeasure to the senior man at the book publishing division, and promotions ceased. He had to buy it back from them. The book is now out of print. Prof. Henry Manne experienced similar treatment with one of his books. After it was published, the president of the firm later told him that he thought the book stank and vowed to kill it.

Other books followed. On the economic trade front, Antony Sutton wrote *National Suicide: Military Aid to the Soviet Union* (Arlington House, 1973), and got himself fired from the ostensibly conservative Hoover Institution. We also have Charles Levinson's *Vodka Cola*, published by the obscure British firm, Gordon and Cremoneosi, New River House, 34 Seymour Road, London, N8 OBE. Levinson is a labor union official (and a Ph.D.). The other book is Joseph Finder's *Red Carpet* (1983), which is now available in a large paperback format: Dominion Press, $9.95. The most documented study is Sutton's *Western Technology and Soviet Economic Development*, a 3-volume study put out by Hoover Institution Press. Sutton proves that 95% of all Soviet technology is either imported from the West or stolen from the West.

Tony Sutton wrote three other books showing how Wall Street millionaires financed Lenin, Hitler, and FDR. He has written a book about what he calls "The Order," which he claims is the conspiracy of conspiracies, with one presently visible outlet, Yale University's secret fraternity, Skull and Bones (into which Vice President Bush and William F. Buckley, Jr., among others—15 per year—have been initiated). He now has people who have access to S&B documents who are now sending him reams of material, some of which he has reprinted. Those of you who have seen the old Glenn Ford T.V. movie, "The Brotherhood of the Bell," may recognize certain aspects of Skull & Bones in that fictional drama. The book is called *America's Secret Establishment* ($19.95). Order from Dominion Press. Sutton continues to uncover numerous groups that work against U.S. interests. He calls them the deaf-mute blindmen.

I don't want to bore you. I'm only trying to show that there is documentation for many of the claims concerning the existence of a well-financed, self-perpetuating, interlocking network of people who use democratic rhetoric and a very sophisticated system of recruiting to gain government favors and protection for their many enterprises (so-called).

My own book, *Conspiracy: A Biblical View*, was published by Crossway Books until certain pressures were put on the firm. They dropped it after one printing, despite the fact that it sold 10,000 copies in eight months. Too hot to handle, it appears. It is available from Dominion Press.

So What?

So, a lot of whats. First a warning. There is a considerable danger that some of you have heard about The Conspiracy before. I have seen a lot of good people become frantic over it. I know of one articulate Ph.D. who has studied The Conspiracy so long, that he now really believes that almost everything on earth is supervised by eight mystic Tibetans. Beware of getting too deeply involved in such investigations. We hear about a "need to know." Respect it. There are limits on what anyone needs to know about secret societies. (Or, "you don't have to eat a whole rotten apple to know it's rotten.")

Second, there are limits on what any group, or interlocking network of self-interested groups, can accomplish. Free markets still occasionally take revenge against those who think they can manipulate them. So do electorates.

Third, the fact that otherwise sensible people don't believe in a conspiracy of any kind doesn't mean a conspiracy isn't (or conspiracies aren't) really there.

Fourth, the elite have "bet the store" on several declining institutions: the international banking system, unbacked paper money, the prestige universities of America, the three major T.V. networks, a handful of newspapers, New York publishing firms, Middle East oil, the Federal bureaucracy, the court system, the public's willingness to pay taxes without cheating excessively, investors' willingness to buy T-bills forever, high real interest rates, and last (but not least) the willingness of the U.S.S.R. to stay in line and behave. It is beginning to look as if they are about to lose their bet. Unfortunately, most of the inventory in their store belongs to us.

What have the elite bet against? This is equally important. Gold, the alternative press (newsletters), the new satellite T.V. networks (especially the Christian ones), private schools (especially the Christian ones), a conservative and anti-mainline denomination revival, the tax revolt, farmers' unrest, bad weather, widespread gun ownership, the political mobilization of newly radicalized Christians (the anti-abortion issue), and the New Right coalition. I think they have bet wrong here, too.

They have also bet against something else, something far more nebulous: a shift in the "climate of opinion." It is this bet, perhaps more than all their others, which is going sour on them. It is therefore our "window of opportunity."

The Climate of Opinion

The manipulators are in trouble—the worst trouble they have been in since 1913. Public opinion is shifting. There is very little they can do about it. The seventy-year romance between the American voter and big government is turning into a series of lovers' quarrels. While the voters still want the government to protect them, and they still want the rich to pay "their fair share," there is a growing realization that the federal government is very close to bankruptcy—economically, intellectually, and above all, morally.

The rise of the neo-conservative movement since 1965 is one indication of this shift. A lot of articulate New York Jews are not 1930s Trotskyites any longer; they are defenders of at least a modified free market, and they are now vociferous critics of Communism of all varieties. All over the landscape these days, intellectuals are singing the praises of decentralization. New Age mystics, former Marxists, best-selling books like Alvin Toffler's *The Third Wave* and John Naisbett's *Megatrends* have all joined the chorus: a new day is a' comin'. Out with central planning, in with local decision-making!

The Left is even making noises about decentralization's benefits, but they just can't pull it off. "Decentralization" is our program, and has always been our side of the debate. I think they are faking it; they still know that they have to have centralized power to maintain their power. They are not ready to decentralize anything they now control. But if they are forced to decentralize, they want to be able to say what and how far. They still want to run the show.

On the other hand, the shift of public opinion may be so powerful that some of them are actually defecting, especially the younger scholarly types. If this continues, today's power elite is headed for the dustbin of history (to use Trotsky's phrase).

The Loss of Faith

They successfully used the pro-government shift in the American climate of opinion after, say, 1880 to further their statist ends. Now that the public has seen the results of this experiment in government centralization, voters are having second thoughts. The old faith in the government as planner is fading.

The manipulators are now beginning to swim upstream intellectually, the way conservatives were forced to swim for three or four generations. The manipulators are not used to swimming upstream. They are out of shape. Intellectually speaking, they resemble Tip O'Neill more than they resemble Mark Spitz. They are used to manipulating public opinion, not fighting it. They are skilled at "going with the flow," not getting swamped by it. They are desperately worried about the growing possibility of finding themselves up liberty creek without a paddle.

They always believe that they can make a deal. Now, sensing that the climate of opinion is shifting, they are tentatively starting to "buy in" to the new right movement. Chase Manhattan Bank in 1983 gave $50,000 to the Heritage Foundation, $15,000 to the Institute for Contemporary Studies, $40,000 to Manhattan Institute for Public Policy, and $10,000 to $20,000 each to several other conservative "public policy" foundations. (Howard Phillips' *Conservative Manifesto* [February 1985], p. 6.) The C.F.R.'s magazine, *Foreign Affairs*, devoted a special issue in early 1985 to "America and the World, 1984." The editor opened it to some conservative critics such as Podhoretz.

Why? Because they are opportunists by conviction and wind testers by training. They understand that the pragmatist's question, "Does it work?" is being answered in the negative, in case after welfare case. The conservatives, especially the neo-conservatives, may not be offering consistent, free market, Constitutional solutions in many instances, but that is not the issue. The issue is, why have intellectuals begun to question the "tried and true" New Deal-Great Society answers? Why are these critics announcing: "tried and false" solutions?

The answer sends chills down the spines of the manipulators: because the solutions that they recommended, and they have long used to create their insulated, government protected world, are visibly failing. As the public, through new intellectual leadership, catches on, the power base of the conspirators will be threatened.

These people are really not that smart. After all, these are the people who, after seventy years, finally got their very own hand-picked man to be President of the United States, and it turned out to be grinning Jimmy, with his beer-loving brother (a paid Libyan agent), his evangelist sister (a pornographer's spiritual counselor)— the President who produced simultaneously the worst foreign policy record in decades (including Salt II, which even the liberal, Democrat-controlled Senate refused to sign), and the most inflationary economic policy in the twentieth century. In short, Jimmy ("Why not the Best?") Carter was visibly the least competent President in U.S. history. That scraping sound we hear may be David Rockefeller scraping the bottom of the barrel.

It doesn't build up a conspirator's self-confidence, does it? This, in my view, is the heart of the matter. The conspirators are losing self-confidence. That is always the beginning of the end: in business, in politics, and in conspiracy. They are now on the run. The emperor has no clothes. I smell fear. What should be our response? Attack! There is only one way to deal with all forms of "conspiracy by manipulation": cut off their funds. Cut off their grants of state privilege. Exposure is not enough. They can live with exposure, though not so easily as without it. But they cannot live without the grants of state power that secure them from the competitive market economy— from the nipping at their heels by brighter, more innovative, and leaner competitors.

It is a wasted effort if we cut off the head of any conspiracy, but leave available to their replacements the raw power of the state, especially the centralized state. Like the hydra-headed monster of Greek mythology, for every head cut off, two more will spring up from the stump. The searing sword of economic liberty must be used to cauterize the monster's open wound and seal it. No more government-guaranteed loans, no more tariffs, no more import quotas, no more racial hiring quotas, no more price supports, no more minimum wage laws, no more compulsory union membership, no more graduated income taxes, and no more fractional reserve banking.

Above all, no more fractional reserve banking. In short, the primary public institutional counter-offensive to all conspiracies is a civil government which is governed by this fundamental truth: there is no such thing as a free lunch. Or to put it bluntly, "You get your hand out of my wallet, and I'll get my hand out of yours." Until the vast majority of voters believe this, and vote in terms of it, conspirators will continue to manipulate the public effectively, and their hands will never get out of our wallets, for they will always tell each of us individually that they are digging even deeper into our neighbor's wallet, and besides, "it's in the public interest."

Can We Win?

When the system goes belly-up, you bet we can win. When the New Deal lies no longer appear to produce the goods, but only "bads," the voters will be ready for a total change, just as the voters in Israel are ready today. That's when our opportunity will come. Our job today is to stick to principles and stick it to our opponents whenever and wherever we can—on principle, by principle, for principle.

Even if we look unpatriotic in the eyes of the defenders of the "status quo," the supporters of "let's make a deal with evil"? Yes. We shouldn't be pessimistic. We've got the proper principles, and eventually these principles are going to triumph. Our knowledge of conspiracies offers us a shovel by which to bury the plans of evil men. This knowledge must not paralyze us with fear concerning "these powerful men." Like Goliath, they are vulnerable, and for similar reasons. Our "shovel" is not to be used to dig our own graves. As God said to Joshua after the death of Moses, and just before the invasion of Canaan, "Be strong, and of a good courage: for unto this people shalt thou divide for an inheritance the land, which I sware unto their fathers to give them. Only be strong and very courageous, that thou mayest observe to do according to the law, which Moses my servant commanded thee: turn not from it to the right hand or to the left, that thou mayest prosper whithersoever thou goest" (Joshua 1:6-7).

The best defense is a good offense. We must take the offensive. And we must be governed by this vision: they are evil and will eventually lose; we are righteous and will eventually win. Therefore: "My hand out of your wallet; your hand out of my wallet; no handouts by the government; and handcuffs for the thieves." I think principled people can and will recapture this country. If you want to see my Bible-based report on this subject, just drop a card or letter to the Institute for Christian Economics, P.O. Box 8000, Tyler, TX 75711, and ask for my special report, "The Sabbath Millennium." We'll send it to you free of charge.

16

THE CASE FOR QUALIFIED OPTIMISM

As always, there are major changes going on. In Western industrial nations, this has been true for 200 years. But these changes are monumental, not just spectacular. These changes point to a change in the type of society we will be living in within 20 years.

When we consider what it takes for a society to restructure its thought and practice, we come back to a chilling word, *revolution*. The revolution always takes place first in the way people think. Then, it manifests itself in the way they act. Finally, it manifests itself in social institutions and politics.

It is clear to everyone that we are already into the first stage, and probably into the second. *The way people think and act today would shock someone who had been in a Communist prison since, say, 1955.* (The Chinese Communists recently released a priest who had been in one of their jails for 30 years.) The magazines on the shelves of many stores would flabbergast him; so would the language in any popular movie or prime T.V. show. Fifteen minutes in front of MTV would put him into shock. (It *still* puts me into shock.) Let him walk the streets of San Francisco for an afternoon to calm him down. It won't.

At the same time, *the intellectual pendulum is swinging back in the direction of conservatism and freedom.* Since 1980, a wealth of new books attacking traditional political liberalism, the welfare State, foreign aid, Marxism, and socialism have poured from the establishment press. Who would have believed that "insider" historian James Billington would publish his stunningly brilliant and exhaustively documented study of the conspiratorial revolutionary movements from 1789 through 1917, *Fire in the Minds of Men* (Basic Books, 1980; $13.95, paperback)? Who would have believed that France's J. F. Revel's scathing attack on Western democracies, *How Democracies Perish*, would be published in the United States by Doubleday ($17.95), and would be a best-seller in Europe? What about Charles Murray's devastating attack on the modern U.S. welfare State, *Losing Ground* (Basic Books, 1984; $23.95)? It is creating a sensation, and sending liberal reviewers into apoplexy. One by one, the reigning liberal myths are collapsing. With them, as we shall see, will go the political institutions built on these myths.

For a bright young person in college today, *the scholarly ammunition to puncture many liberal myths is easily available*, although aging tenured professors are not about to assign such books as required reading. The self-confidence of liberal intellectuals is fading, and I believe it is fading rapidly. *When your opponents' self-confidence goes, the primary battle is over; only a mopping-up operation lies ahead.* This is what the Left recognized in conservatives at the turn of the century. This is why they won. We tend to forget that the era of what I call *the Power State*, as an intellectual force, has lasted less than a century.

The Problem With Revolutions

If we are serious conservatives, we recognize that revolutions have almost always centralized political power. They lead to social disruptions, which in turn lead to more demands for the State to bring order. In late nineteenth-century Russia, as Billington and others have shown, double agents pressured the revolutionaries to increase terrorism against the State. Then the police could demand increased powers to combat revolutionaries—and so on, until the Russian revolution. In some cases, we still aren't sure where the loyalties of these agents really lay. Maybe they didn't know for sure.

Frederick Engels, Karl Marx's partner and bankroller, wrote this concerning revolutions:

. . . the anti-authoritarians demand that the authoritarian political state be abolished at one stroke, even before the social conditions that gave birth to it have been destroyed. They demand that the first act of the social revolution shall be the abolition of authority. Have these gentlemen ever seen a revolution? A revolution is certainly the most authoritarian thing there is; it is the act whereby one part of the population imposes its will upon the other part by means of rifles, bayonets, and common-authoritarian means, if such there be at all; and if the victorious party does not want to have fought in vain, it must maintain this rule by means of the terror which its arms inspire in the reactionaries.

Our goal is not revolution; it is social, moral, and religious *transformation*. If violence must come (and I am not convinced that it must), then what we want is what we had in 1776, a *conservative counter-revolution*, within the framework of legitimate local institutions. The states made war on Britain; the revolutionaries did not act as lawless individuals. The militia made war, not independent revolutionary bands of thugs. A citizen army won that war. That's why the militia and the Second Amendment are still crucial to our liberties. (The best book I've seen on this: Morgan Norval (ed.), *The Militia in 20th Century America*, $9.95: order from Dominion Press, P.O. Box 8204, Ft. Worth, TX 76124.)

What we face is an entrenched Establishment which is doing endless deals with our mortal enemies. Until the policies of this political, academic, and media Establishment are at last repudiated by the American public, we will continue to drift into nuclear blackmail. The question is: *When will those policies be perceived as suicidal by the voters?*

Answer: *not until the economy fails to produce the promised goodies at low cost.* People are pocketbook oriented. Sophisticated theories are irrelevant to them. What they want is the goods. As long as the system delivers the goods, they will not rebel.

Thus, the argument in favor of positive social and political change rests on the presupposition that big government cannot deliver the goods forever, that big government is parasitic and eventually must drain the host, which in this case is the middle class voter.

In other words, as long as the system seems to be working, the best we can hope for is *time to prepare ourselves* for the period when it will no longer be working properly. This means economic preparation. It also means intellectual, institutional, and even political preparation.

The Quiet Political Transformation

What can we do about politics? Plenty. Let me give you an example. A recent survey by the Republican Party revealed that out of the 3,300 counties in the United States, the Republican Party has functioning regional organizations in only 1,300 of them, and effective organizations in about 300. Given the fate of Mr. Mondale, it seems reasonable to presume that the Democrats are not significantly better organized.

These empty counties are ripe for a takeover by dedicated conservatives who are in the fight for the duration. I know of several conservative alliances that are now actively beginning to establish

Republican Party organizations in these unrepresented counties. They are mobilizing previously unregistered and non-political Christians who have little experience but who are getting the political picture. Since something is preferable to nothing, the national Parties will welcome newcomers. But these newcomers will not be taking orders from national headquarters. This is a political revolution in the making. The question is, *who will be educating these newcomers?* That's where my work comes in. I am doing my best to work with the leaders of various Christian organizations in the area of Christian economics. The market demand for such information is far higher than it was even five years ago. There are things going on that I am not going to make public. Let's just say that there is light at the end of our tunnel — not big government's tunnel.

The Reagan euphoria undercut all direct mail appeals for funds. The older right wing organizations have been out of the picture since 1981. Now even the "New Right" organizations are hurting. The money isn't coming in any more. *This has created an historic opportunity for new conservative groups to step into a vacuum.*

When the economy begins to unravel, as it will, there will be demand for new answers from new groups that have not been tarred and feathered with the supply-side economics fiasco. The supply-siders became proponents of "temporary" budget deficits ("deficits don't matter") and loose money policies by the Federal Reserve System. Supply-side economics is dying, monetarism is in retreat politically (though a revival of inflation will help to resuscitate it), and there is nothing on the conservative horizon to replace them. This means that any new approach has got to make use of the older approach which has deliberately been ignored by professional economists, Austrian economics or some modification thereof. The hard core anti-statists have got the only "clean" theory in town. This is one reason why the supply-siders and monetarists have opposed the Austrians; the Austrians want a fully redeemable gold coin standard and little or no fractional reserve banking. These two heresies cannot be tolerated by institutionalized economists — and most economists *do* need to be institutionalized.

In other words, the political change we are hoping for has got to come as a result of *new political blood* being injected into the sick body politic. New ideas, new people, new vision: this is what it will take. This is also what's coming.

In 1979, I did not see it coming. Nobody did. Every warm body that could be dragged to the polls was already in somebody's hip pocket. But there was one exception: the fundamentalist church members. Instinctively conservative, they have been out of politics as a separate force since 1930. This voting block was unregistered. *Something like 10 million unregistered fundamentalists constitute the largest swing vote in the country.* Now, at long last, skilled political amateurs are beginning to get them registered. Training programs are in the wings. Pat Robertson's flirtation with a run for the Presidency has helped to get fundamentalist groups to rethink their long hostility to "getting involved in politics—the things of this world." A new voting bloc will alter American politics if there are major crises in the 1990s.

Crises are going to transform the political scene. The political professionals haven't seen this coming. Robertson's move toward politics is going to get millions of instinctively conservative but previously apathetic voters to the polls. And he is going to be the central figure in *the training of a whole new generation of conservative activists.* The liberals will be astounded, then outraged, then (eventually) conciliatory. Their religion is political, and when we have sufficient votes to become the key swing voting bloc, they will come, hat in hand, to cut deals. They always do.

It is interesting that the "New Right" organizations spotted the shift in 1980. They have spent time and money in training the leadership of the "New Christian Right" leaders. They now see these new potential constituents as the key to the future. There are "networks" forming among many of the New Right and New Christian Right organizations. The New Right provides the expertise, and the New Christian Right provides the bodies. This alliance will continue, and as they get the training, the Christian forces will become more independent. This process will be complete within a decade, and the major political implications of this shift should be visible by the 1992 election.

Those of us who are involved are keeping our mouths shut about the details. But I want you to understand that a major transformation of American politics has begun, and you will begin to see results during the next President's term in office. As the Establishment prescriptions visibly disintegrate, the new alliance will begin to bear fruit.

Fruits and Nuts

The problem I see is that with amateurs, you get a significant proportion of nuts. Bearing fruit requires that we bear with a few nuts. This was true in the early days of every successful political revolution. The Fabians had their share of weirdos. So did the Marxists. The point is, *amateurs are amateurish*. They will come up with crackpot schemes continually. There is only one sure defense: better theoretical foundations. You have to be able to spot nonsense.

Keep two invisible parrots on your shoulders. The first one will be taught only three words, "supply and demand." When you get confused about the logic of any proposed economic scheme, consult him. The second one will know only four words, "Who pays the freight?" When you're in doubt about the wisdom of any reasonable sounding proposal that gets by the first parrot, consult the second.

The other major threat is the rise of armed nuts who call conservatives to mindless action. We are already seeing this. They will be matched by the reappearance of Weathermen terrorists and other armed radical lunatics. The thin veneer of social stability is wearing through in Europe now; we're next. It is imperative that you stay far removed from those who call for armed violence. Remember the Russian revolutionary experience: the symbiotic relationship between the terrorists and the police. There are "agents provocateurs," as well as outright nuts. They can wave flags as well as the next guy, whether red, white, and blue, or red, or black, or white with one or another variation of a cross on it.

What we need to understand is that *short of surrender to the Soviet Union*, there is still plenty of peaceful, steady, long-term political work to be done that involves nothing more violent than a voter registration training program. I am assuming that even surrender will be invisible, and that our national leaders will capitulate to blackmail, but do it quietly. If this happens, the door to political victory is still open.

We have valid intellectual alternatives. The longer private schools and home schools do their work, the larger the growing constituency that will respond favorably to a call to return to Constitutional restraints on civil government. The public schools' days are numbered. So is the ideology of state power.

We also have valid institutional alternatives. I don't just mean political institutions. I mean small businesses that Americans are still permitted to start. I mean voluntary charities that alone will be able to "pick up the slack" when the printing presses destroy the monetary unit, or when price controls strangle it. If we don't have alternatives — working alternatives — to offer, then we will lose the argument for freedom. You can't fight something with nothing. *Power flows to those who are willing to accept responsibility.*

Where We Are Winning

I have already mentioned the major area of victory: private education. The home school movement is exploding. Parents are teaching their children at home. Through at least the fifth grade, most mothers can handle the job, except with foreign languages. (Besides, few schools offer elementary school children foreign languages, except in Europe, where people actually learn to speak foreign languages.)

The *conventional* military situation is universally grim. The Soviets have us beaten in every category, from nuclear strike capability to conventional land and sea forces to insurgency and counter-insurgency tactics. Money will not solve any of these problems; only a new strategy, coupled with new technology, can possibly work.

Yet even though the Western industrial nations have steadily retreated, Third World victims of tyranny are now beginning to resist. In Angola, Mozambique, Afghanistan, and Nicaragua, full-scale military campaigns are being fought against Marxist governments. These liberation movements are beginning to sap the Soviet empire of its resources. Only the inactivity of the United States — or worse, active support of the Marxist targets of liberation — has saved these regimes from a successful revolution by the disenfranchised. There is no doubt that such movements are unnerving to the Soviets, for they have not had to face determined opponents who use guerrilla tactics against Soviet surrogates. The Soviets have to bail out these inefficient, faltering nations, and the bills are rising.

Meanwhile, the Soviets now face the really devastating threat to their system: the computer revolution. They need miniaturization if they are ever to compete in outer space, and they can only steal it; they can't produce it on a mass scale. Besides, the thought of citizens with computers, data banks, printers, and similar basic tools of research and productivity petrifies the leadership, which is already a study in calcified geriatrics. The whole idea behind socialism is to centralize planning, and therefore to centralize information. Computers decentralize both planning and information.

The speed of computer developments is staggering. The power of a 1987 $4,000 computer that sits on a desk is vastly greater than the power of a $100,000 computer in 1980. I bought a used computer for about $30,000 in 1981 that cost $6,000 a year just to insure against breakdowns. The firm that produced it, Data General, has almost disappeared, despite the fact that in 1983 a best-selling book was written about the development of a now-obsolete computer by the firm, *The Soul of a New Machine.*

A primitive version of the WordPerfect word processing program that I am using today cost $7,500 in 1981, and it worked only on a $30,000 (used price) Data General computer; you can buy the far more powerful version today from a New York computer mail order store for $190. It works on an $800 (new price) computer. These advances in computer technology and programs continue to escalate.

A "Dick Tracy" type of wristwatch-sized telephone now exists in an experimental form. By transmitting a signal to a nearby cellular telephone switching system, and from there up to a satellite 23,000 miles above the earth, a person can telephone anywhere in the world. Larger versions of such phones are now commercially available; they fit into an inside coat pocket. You can walk down the street and chat with someone 12,000 miles away.

Space-based technologies for growing almost flawless crystals in a dust-free, zero-gravity environment promise to transform electronics in the late 1990s. The computer revolution will make another major leap forward when these crystals become available commercially. Fiber optics will also begin to transform communications, replacing copper wire. Fantastic new superconductors of energy have appeared since early 1986; they operate at very cold temperatures, but far higher than the near-absolute zero temperatures that were required to make them superconductors as recently as 1985.

What about rare industrial or strategic metals? We desperately need South Africa for the moment, but not beyond the year 2000. Ben Bova's amazing book, *The High Road,* tells the story of the rare elements on the moon. Low gravity means that metals mined on the moon will be relatively cheap to get into earth orbit, and from there into goods manufactured in space. There is even a more revolutionary possibility: the asteroid belt. Nuclear-powered rockets could fly out and bring one back. The mining potential is, quite literally, astronomical.

We are on the verge of the most spectacular economic transformation in history. When I say we, I mean the United States. The Soviet Union will not participate, unless our leaders sell them the goods or give them the goods.

What this means is that strategically, the Soviets have bet on the wrong horse . . . unless they launch a first strike before we get our defense in space. But that's a high risk proposition. The Soviets will become little more than a Third World nation with an expensive, technologically backward military force. Their economy will never catch up to the West. If. . . . *If* the United States abandons the the-ology of the power State. *If* the United States abandons the policies of borrow now, borrow tomorrow, and pay off with bad money. *If* the United States stops sending our high-tech goods and food to the Soviet Union. *If* the United States goes into high gear in the Star Wars project. *If* the United States gets taxes down and spending lower.

We are in a position for a new birth of liberty. The profit potential for those who don't falter will be spectacular. The basic moral rules will stay the same, but the avenues for profit will be completely un-familiar to most people.

The Power Religion

We are in a situation that is overwhelmingly positive, if men are left free, and if the nation is defended. The trouble is, this nation's political leaders, and far too many of the voters, have been devoted adherents to what I call the power religion. But compared to the Communists, we are pikers.

In the Old Testament, we read story after story of what hap-pened to Israel when the people adopted the fertility religions called Baalism. Their leaders became bribe-seekers and power-seekers. Then the nation would fall to an outside invading nation. In short, God demonstrated to them time after time, *if you adopt the gods of your enemies, you will be forced to serve those gods.* If you adopt a rival god, you thereby adopt the rival god's society. They were slave societies, and the Hebrews kept going into slavery. They kept abandoning the God of the Bible, adopting the *power religion* of their enemies.

The power religion is a faith in raw power—terrorism, central economic planning, military might—that says that man's highest goal is the suppression of other people's liberties. It is man's task to control everything, and an elite's task to control other men.

This religion has been with us from the day that Cain slew Abel. The most important ancient confrontation between the power relig-ion and its chief rival, the *ethics religion*, took place in Egypt about 3500 years ago. It was the conflict between Moses and Pharaoh.

Bible commentators have not really understood what was going on. What we see in the Exodus was a confrontation between the most powerful bureaucracy in man's history (until the early twentieth century) and an oppressed people. The state had made slaves of the Hebrews, and the Hebrews for the most part were unwilling to take any risks to change their condition. It sounds like most voters today!

What Moses did was to prove for all time that *no matter how powerful a political religion is, it can be broken by principled opposition.* The account of the Exodus in the Book of Exodus provides us with the classic example of the inescapable doom of all power-oriented empires. It takes time, but the collapse eventually comes.

The Soviet Union is the most consistent worshipper of the power religion since Egypt. What we are seeing in our day is the most important confrontation between the ethics religion and the power religion since the days of Rome. Each side has a doctrine of victory. Each side has a doctrine of the millennium, or kingdom of peace; the debate is over whose kingdom it is: the kingdom of God or the kingdom of man. Each side has a doctrine of regeneration. Christianity teaches that men are regenerated by grace resulting in faith in Christ, and this leads them to begin to serve as "salt" or "salve" in the society at large. The Soviets, being environmental determinists, believe (following Marx) that social orders are regenerated through bloody revolution, and then an elite ruling class will re-educate the population, thereby regenerating individuals. It is salvation by law — statist law.

To the extent that America's establishment has adopted some version of environmental determinism and elitist central planning, they have adopted the power religion. No wonder they are afraid to confront the Soviets. The Soviets are more faithful to the tenets of the power religion. They use terror and suppression without guilt, unlike our home-grown power religionists, who have a trace of charity left in them.

This is why *the fight we face today is a moral and religious fight.* We are being taxed endlessly to support the chosen beneficiaries of our leaders' version of the power religion. This is the religion of the major institutions of our day, especially the universities.

There is a third religion, the escapist religion. Until the advent of the humanist counter-culture after 1964, the major practitioners were the "eat, meet, and retreat" fundamentalists. No longer is this the case. The fundamentalists are learning about politics about the time that the dope-heads of the sixties are becoming hedonistic, present-oriented "yuppies." The escapists are always allied with the power religionists. The Hebrews in Egypt were allied to their taskmasters and against Moses. This was true even in the wilderness. But eventually Joshua's generation takes over. The escapists die in the wilderness.

What I'm arguing is that *in our day, we are seeing the last of the Christian escapists dying in the wilderness.* The confrontation looms ahead: Canaanites vs. Joshua's generation, the power religion vs. the ethics religion.

And let us not forget God's words to Joshua before the fight began: "Only be thou strong and very courageous, that thou mayest observe to do according to all the law, which Moses my servant commanded thee: turn not from it to the right hand or to the left, that thou mayest prosper whithersoever thou goest" (Joshua 1:7). Joshua repeated this warning to his followers in his old age (Joshua 23:6). The point is clear: *right makes might.* Ethics leads to dominion; power-seeking leads to defeat.

Remember also the words of Proverbs 13:22(b): ". . . the wealth of the sinner is laid up for the just."

This is why I don't think the Soviets are going to take the risk of trying to blow us up. They will probably attempt nuclear blackmail before this generation of two-bit power religionists gets off the political stage, but I think they will get too involved militarily elsewhere. A positive moral change is in the works, however weak. *The free ride for the power religionists is over.*

That's why I think there are legitimate reasons for *optimism*. Not blind optimism; after all, the Hebrews got *into* slavery before they got *out*. Today, there is a new movement in this country away from the worship of power and the politics of envy. I think we may get *a stay of execution . . .* if we shape up *fast!*

17

PROTECTING YOUR SOURCE

> Lay not up for yourselves treasures upon earth, where moth and
> rust doth corrupt, and where thieves break through and steal: But lay
> up for yourselves treasures in heaven, where neither moth nor rust
> doth corrupt, and where thieves do not break through nor steal: For
> where your treasure is, there will you heart be also. (Matthew 6:19-21)

Like so many conservative Americans, I bought a copy of
Aleksandr Solzhenitsyn's *Gulag Archipelago*. Also like many conservative Americans, I put off reading it. But in 1978 I devoted Sunday
afternoons to knocking off a couple of hundred pages, which means
about a hundred pages, plus a nap, plus other interruptions, plus a
weekend skipped, etc. But line by line, chapter by chapter, I plowed
through it. It was a most rewarding exercise in self-discipline on my
part. I learned things that my courses in Russian history and Soviet
government never quite communicated.

The Gulag Archipelago will remain a classic. If any book is read in a
hundred years that appeared in our generation, it will be this one.
Or, if things go badly, if any book is prohibited in a hundred years, it
will be this one. What sticks in the mind—my mind, anyway—is the
extent of the insanity and destructiveness of the Soviet regime.
Those who survived did so on a seemingly random basis. A few people ran away when they learned of their impending arrest, but very
few. No one resisted. No one yelled, screamed, or beat up the arresting KGB officials. They went meekly to the slaughter. Jews in
Germany, kulaks in Russia, citizens in every totalitarian state seem
to have this one thing in common: they do not make a scene, even
when their worlds are collapsing around them. And the monsters
who run the State, meaning other faceless citizens under the command of truly demonic elites, take every advantage of this meekness.

Thomas Molnar, the conservative scholar, suffered under the regimes of both the Nazis and the Communists. He once made a very significant observation. He said that the way you could sometimes escape from a Nazi-dominated village was to dress up as if you were going out for a stroll. You and your wife and children would create no unusual appearance. You might even tip your hat at the military policeman or other official. With nothing more than the clothes on your back, you would march down to the train station and buy a ticket for the next town down the line. Station by station, you could get your way closer to the border. Then you could risk a silent crossing in the dark of the night, or by bribing a guard. Significantly, he noted, those with lots of possessions seldom took this approach in the early days of military law. They would sit in their homes and hope for the best. This is exactly what Solzhenitsyn notes. The result was too often the loss of everything, including personal liberty.

When I was studying economic history in graduate school, our professor, Herbert Heaton, told us this fascinating story. One friend of his in England, before Heaton came to this country, was a Jewish economic historian. (I'm operating from a 1966 memory: I have forgotten his name.) The man had been working on a long-term study in German economic history. When the Nazis came to power, he had forebodings about his future. From then on, he made carbon copies of every document he typed up for his files. He sent the carbon copies, piece by piece, to Sir John Clapham, the British economic historian. He trusted Clapham not to steal his material. Finally, since the Nazis allowed people to leave Germany, including Jews, the scholar left. He was not allowed to take anything with him. Few Jews took this route to freedom, although of course several thousand did, but this was hardly a majority of those who had the opportunity; it was a mere fraction. When he arrived in England, he had his notes. He could continue his studies. Most of his fellow refugee scholars had to leave everything behind. This included Ludwig von Mises, who had to abandon his library, a very difficult thing for any scholar to do. Both these men enjoyed fruitful careers later on, however, which those who perished under Nazi rule could not do.

What am I getting at? Simple: a crisis can overtake any of us in our tracks at any time. The flooding in the hills of southern California in 1978, the freezing in the Midwest and Northeast, and similar disasters can sweep unsuspecting people away. Their hopes, dreams, and careful plans do not avail them if the crisis is great enough. An all encompassing disaster waits for no one to get his house in order. That wood stove and year's supply of food at home could not help those caught in the blizzard on the Ohio turnpikes in 1978.

Solzhenitsyn describes in detail a long-forgotten event in the late 1920s. He calls it "gold fever." This was a period in which Stalin was consolidating his position by exterminating his former colleagues in the Presidium—the standard practice of violent revolutions to consume their founders—and to centralize the nation's production system. The New Economic Policy (NEP), inaugurated by Lenin to reverse the starvation of the "war communism period," which started in 1922 and lasted until this period of Stalin's rule, had decentralized small businesses, thereby encouraging increased output. Solzhenitsyn writes:

The famous gold fever began at the end of 1929, only the fever gripped not those looking for gold but those from whom it was being shaken loose. The particular feature of this new, "gold" wave was that the GPU was not actually accusing these rabbits of anything, and was perfectly willing not to send them off to Gulag country, but wished only to take away their gold by main force. So the prisons were packed, the interrogators were worn to a frazzle, but the transit prisons, prisoner transports, and camps received only relatively minor reinforcements.

Who was arrested in this "gold" wave? All those who, at one time or another, fifteen years before, had a private "business," had been involved in retail trade, had earned wages at a craft, and could have, according to the GPU's deductions, hoarded gold. But it so happened that they often had no gold. They had put their money into real estate or securities, which had melted away or been taken away in the Revolution, and nothing remained. They had high hopes, of course, in arresting dental technicians, jewelers, and watch repairman. . . . Nothing—neither proletarian origin nor revolutionary services—served as a defense against a gold denunciation. All were arrested, all were crammed into GPU cells in numbers no one had considered possible up to then—but that was all too good: they would cough it up all the sooner! . . . Only one thing was important: Give us your gold, viper! The state needs gold and you don't. The interrogators had neither voice nor strength left to threaten and torture; they had one universal method: feed the prisoners nothing but salty food and give them no water. Whoever coughed up gold got water! One gold piece for a cup of fresh water. . . . If you in fact had not gold, then your situation was hopeless. You would be beaten, burned, tortured, and steamed to the point of death or until they finally came to believe you (Vol. 1, pp. 52-53).

The Chinese Communists used a different technique in the early years of their revolution. The situation there was different. When a Communist force would enter a village, they would try to get access to weapons. This was during the Japanese war period. The details are provided by Raymond de Jaegher, a Belgian Roman Catholic priest, who was a Jesuit missionary in China at the time, and his co-author, Irene Corbally Kuhn, in their neglected and important book, *The Enemy Within* (1952). I hope that their account eventually gets a wide hearing in the anti-gun control camp. They wrote:

Every Chinese family that had any property at all, even just their cooking utensils, their bedrolls, a few primitive farm tools, yearned for a gun. A gun meant protection. Farmers banded together to share common ownership of one rifle; wealthier farmers and landowners had a few rifles. Indeed, rifles were a rich medium of exchange, and in those times people preferred them to cash.

The Communists needed all the rifles they could lay their hands on beyond what they were allowed to have legally, if they were to increase in power and numbers. Persons were arrested on the slightest pretext and forced to pay a certain number of rifles. In fact, everyone arrested was faced with the alternative of handing over rifles or being shot. Always the people were punished for misdemeanors, big crimes, or no crimes at all by being fined in arms instead of money, a typical Communist trick which was used as part of an ascending spiral of ever-increasing demands to achieve maximum control over the population.

When the Communists first arrived and took such pains to make a good impression on the populace, they stressed their determination to save China from the Japanese. They appealed to people for funds over and above regular taxes, for a "war fund" and "to help the government." Many rich men, seeking to win favor with the authorities, contributed to the fund and then and there unwittingly sealed their doom, even as did good decent citizens who gave willingly and generously, often at great sacrifice. The Communists merely waited for the right moment and then applied the screws.

It was simple procedure. They would call in a rich man who had given fifty dollars in the drive to "help the government."

"You are rich," a Communist officer would tell him, fixing him with an accusing eye. "Your contribution of fifty dollars to your government is not enough. You must now give arms. Bring ten rifles here tomorrow." He would name the hour, dismiss the man, and put his chop on the order.

No one could buy rifles easily in China in those days, and since the man's life depended on his getting them, a black market quickly developed. The Communists encouraged this, as they encourage any illegal or irregular enterprise which will serve their purpose. A rifle worth fifty dollars on Monday then acquired a greatly inflated value on Tuesday; when the desperate man finally tracked down his quota he had spent a small fortune.

As the weeks went by and more and more such fines were levied by the Communists, it was seen that the process was continuous. The man who was fined ten rifles at first was neither shot nor imprisoned at that time, but just when he began to breathe easily once more, he would be arrested again and fined ten more rifles. It was much harder for him to get the guns the second time and the deal cost him much more. By this time, too, he knew he was only buying a little time and that he would have to resign himself to a third arrest and a third demand, and so on, until one fine day . . .

In this way the Communists got a fine haul of arms (pp. 42-43).

The story of how the Communists expropriated a class of people simultaneously expanding their control over the population by disarming it, is not something to be ignored. We have to ask ourselves, what would we have done? Would we have left town as soon as we saw what the goals of the invaders really were? Would we have left after that first arrest? Or would we have sat around quietly, waiting for things to get better, hoping that the demands on our dwindling resources would finally be reduced? Think about it.

Here is an almost universal fact: people do exactly what the Chinese landed gentry did. They allow themselves to be skinned without a whimper. Why do we believe that we would act differently?

The Soft Underbelly

Totalitarians rely heavily, confidently, and continually upon their understanding of human nature. They realize that men are incurably habit-oriented, willing to suffer almost any disruptions in their wealth or freedom if they are permitted to believe that the basic outline of their lives will be left unimpeded. If the authorities are very careful to give the next victim the impression that today's victim may be the last, or that there are other victims in line, then most people most of the time will sit quietly and wait to be sheared. This reduces the costs of control to a minimum. In that graphic phrase of Solzhenitsyn's, "A submissive sheep is a find for a wolf."

Part of any serious program of economic and political survival is that of mental and psychological conditioning. It is not sufficient to stock up on your supplies of dehydrated fruits and gold coins. The rifle you bought is no better than your determination to use it and your ability to use it. This means that you have to have some sort of guideline about when and under what circumstances to use it. In a time of true terror, which I hope never comes, but which cannot be dismissed lightly, each man must have a mental line drawn, over which his opponent cannot step at zero risk. The drawing of that line is probably more important than other physical preparations. Where a man's treasure is, there is his heart. What am I getting at? Simple: all of your preparations should be aimed at preserving your freedom first, and only secondarily aimed at protecting your wealth. Your wealth is simply a tool for expanding your productivity under freedom. Your wealth must not be allowed to capture you, to chain you to the ground while the wolves plan your demise. Get this into your mind early: your wealth is your tool to utilize freedom, not your enemy's tool of dominion over you. The soft underbelly of America is here: our inability to understand the proper use of wealth. We cling to our wealth as if it could save us in a major crisis. As toolmakers, we have learned to worship the products of our hands-silent gods that neither speak nor give counsel.

We have confused means with ends, and we have worshipped means. So did those Chinese landowners.

Yet no bureaucracy is perfect. There were and always will be ways out, although few people find them. Solzhenitsyn's account of Andrei Pavel is instructive:

On the other hand, the NKVD did come to get the Latvian Andrei Pavel near Orsha. But he didn't open the door; he jumped out the window, escaped, and shot straight to Siberia. And even though he lived under his own name, it was clear from his documents that he had come from Orsha, he was never arrested, nor summoned to the Organs [security system], nor subjected to any suspicion whatsoever. After all, search for wanted persons falls into three categories; All-Union, republican, and provincial. And the pursuit of nearly half of those arrested in those epidemics would have been confined to the provinces. A person marked for arrest by virtue of chance circumstances, such as a neighbor's denunciation, could be easily replaced by another neighbor. Others, like Andrei Pavel, who found themselves in a trap or in an ambushed apartment by accident, and who were bold enough to escape immediately, before they could be questioned, were never caught and never charged; while those who stayed behind to await justice got a term in prison. And the overwhelming majority-almost all-behaved just like that: without any spirit, helplessly, with a sense of doom (Vol. 1, pp. 11-12).

He adds this footnote one page later:

And how we burned in the camps later, thinking: What would things have been like if every Security operative, when he went out at night to make an arrest, had been uncertain whether he would return alive and had to say good-bye to his family? Or if, during periods of mass arrests, as for example in Leningrad, when they arrested a quarter of the entire city, people had not simply sat in their lairs, paling with terror at every bend of the downstairs door and at every step on the staircase, but had understood they had nothing left to lose and had boldly set up in the downstairs hall an ambush of half a dozen people with axes, hammers, pokers, or whatever else was at hand: After all, you knew ahead of time that those bluecaps were out at night for no good purpose. And you could be sure ahead of time that you'd be cracking the skull of a cutthroat. Or what about the Black Maria sitting out there on the street with one lonely chauffeur-what if it had been driven off or its tires spiked? The Organs would quickly have suffered a shortage of officers and transport, and notwithstanding all of Stalin's thirst, the cursed machine would have ground to a halt.

If . . . If . . . We didn't love freedom enough. And even more—we had no awareness of the real situation. We spent ourselves in one unrestrained outburst in 1917, and then we hurried to submit. We submitted with pleasure! . . . We purely and simply deserved everything that happened afterward.

The Three Worlds

If a person is to be successful in the possible scenarios before us, he has to live in three worlds. I am not speaking of the much-touted "multinational person." The world will not be rebuilt by multinational nomads, however useful their tax-haven-protected newsletters may be. I am speaking of something much more fundamental. The three worlds are, in order of importance (greatest to least important):

1. The residence of the heart (where your treasure is . . .)
2. The residence of the body
3. The future residence of the body

Why couldn't the Europeans known by Molnar have just walked out of their homes and headed for the border? Why couldn't the Russians have acted like Andrei Pavel? Why didn't those Chinese landlords just walk away from the Chinese Communists to join Chiang's forces? After all, that's what the Red Chinese did in the 1934 Long March, when they escaped Chiang by walking thousands of miles to isolation and safety. I think the difference between the landlords and

Mao was the location of their treasure. Mao's treasure was in an ideal of a Communist revolution. His heart was in the utopian future. So he walked away. He escaped, survived, and lived to return in force. He knew where the treasures of his enemies were buried: in their traditional way of life. So he dug up their treasures, family by family, until there was nothing left of that traditional way of life. Hoping to save their lives, his enemies forfeited their lives and treasures. They would live or die in Mao's kingdom, at the discretion of the Communists.

We must live in the present, where we make our daily income. We have to build in terms of what we have now and where our responsibilities are. We have to hope that our present circumstances will not be disrupted. We have a lot of treasure buried here. But to insure our own safety, we have got to rethink the meaning of treasure. It had better not be in bricks and mortar. How many alumni have financed the destruction of capitalism by blindly (and not so blindly) contributing to their old alma mater to buy a little phony immortality, the Crittendon J. Armbuster economics building? It is not bricks and mortar, but the use of bricks and mortar, that should capture our imaginations. Andrei Pavel knew this when he jumped out of the window and headed for Siberia. The present is worth only part of our sacrifice. We hold our possession of the present only on a lease, not as a permanent title.

We have to live in terms of the likely future, not our hoped-for future. We have to sacrifice present enjoyments in order to build up the survival capital we expect to use in the future. That capital had better be mobile, and if not mobile, then at least isolated. One tank full of gasoline away we should have at least a spot of ground, a septic tank, a well, and a building, if only a used mobile home bought at a steep discount for cash from someone living in a trailer court nearby. (The equity in a mobile home drops to about $4,000 after seven years, so it's not that great of an investment.)

Conclusion

You dare not put your trust in things. Things are means to entertain personal ends. Let them capture your heart, and you have offered crucial leverage to the tyrants of the world. Things can be confiscated anyway; sacrificing for your future for the sake of them, only to be removed from them, is the very act which The Gulag

Archipelago warns against. Mobility is a more important asset for short-run maneuvering, since isolation and invisibility may be initially dependent upon mobility. But in the long run, nothing can protect a person from the external crises of life. Robbers break in, and rust erodes. You can't take it with you. But if you have it buried in the wrong place, it sure can take you with it.

CONCLUSION

You have read a book which some people will regard as pessimistic, while others will see it as optimistic. For the long haul, I am an optimist. For the short haul, I am a pessimist. I see a coming shaking of the foundations of Western civilization. I see the AIDS plague, Soviet expansion, the international debt bomb, the uncontrollable U.S. Federal debt, mass inflation, and ever-greater government attempts to control our lives. I also see a major change coming: loss of faith in the present system. As the defects of socialism and economic interventionism become visible to everyone, many of the voters will abandon faith in the all-promising state. This is optimistic.

To catch the attention of a nation of pragmatists, there must be a huge crisis. People who believe that anything that "works" is valid have adopted a false religion. To persuade them to change their minds, we must be able to point to massive failure of the present world order. A series of major crises will provide all the evidence we need. This is pessimistic.

Unfortunately, evidence of failure is not enough to produce positive change. People must know *why* the present system has failed. They must understand that it is morally perverse and economically inefficient. In a major crisis, every lunatic fringe group will try to persuade the voters that their solutions are the only ones that will work. It will be difficult for people living in real fear to make accurate analyses and decisions concerning what went wrong and what needs to be done. This is why it is important for principled people to study the economy well in advance of the crises. They must be confident that what they believe is morally correct; only then will they have the courage to persuade people in a crisis situation.

This book is partly about investing and partly about economic principle. Without economic principle, profits will accomplish little. People must understand why they are investing one way rather than

185

another. They must know why they have adopted "crisis investing" strategies: because crises really are coming, if I am correct about cause and effect, meaning *moral* cause and effect, not just economic cause and effect.

The present state-controlled economy is immoral. It uses force and the threat of force to take assets from one group and give them to another. It is the theology that rests on a perverse version of the eighth commandment: "Thou shalt not steal, except by majority vote." Today's economy is based on faith in the state as an agency of social salvation. Such a faith is bound to fail. We must begin to disengage ourselves from dependence on the state and its monopoly agencies. We cannot do this perfectly without becoming hermits, but we must do a lot more than most people have done in the past.

The real issue is morality. If we fail to persuade others in the coming crises that a return to faith in God and faith in freedom is the only hope of humanity, then a dark age lies ahead of us. The scourges of God—war, pestilence, and famine—will accompany any escalation of state power in our lives. It is time to make a decision, as it was in Elijah's day. If Baal be God, then follow him. But if the Lord God of the Bible is God, then follow Him (I Kings 18:21).

INDEX